PRAISE FOR *A JOURNEY THROUGH THE WORLD OF LEVITICUS*

"Scarlata proves himself a gifted and insightful guide as he carefully unpacks the meaning and significance of Leviticus in its ancient context, in light of the New Testament and Christian faith, and for contemporary realities. . . . In the end, Scarlata's book achieves what the book of Leviticus itself wants to achieve: a re-sacralization of our world, which is indeed 'crammed with heaven.' Take and read!"

—*Brent A. Strawn*, Duke University

"In this unlikely yet thoroughly engaging book, Scarlata refocuses us on holiness as the heartbeat of community life, in contemporary society no less than in the world of the Bible. Scarlata sees the crucial point that most Christian biblical scholars and readers of the Bible have missed: that the embodied theology of Leviticus is indispensable for making a living connection between the reality of God and our concrete human lives."

—*Ellen F. Davis*, Duke Divinity School

"'God in everything.' Mark Scarlata calls for a re-sacralization of the world in this Christian reading of Leviticus. He shows how features of the book that have led it to be neglected by Christians—purity, food laws, sacrifice, and holiness—are central to the religion of ancient Israel. They can also inform a modern Christian attitude to the created world."

—*John Barton*, University of Oxford, emeritus

"Leviticus attests to an alternative world that has God's holiness at its center. Scarlata . . . shows us why attentiveness to an alternative world of holiness is urgent among us. . . . It is clear enough now that our present path of technological exploitation, predatory debt, and individualistic consumerism is not sustainable. If you may be wondering about a very different way to live well, free, and responsibly in the world, you may indeed find Scarlata's wise discussion particularly helpful and illuminating."

—Walter Brueggemann, Columbia Theological Seminary

"Scarlata has made Leviticus great again—making it plainly understandable and relevant to everything we care about and do today. With scholarly insight and pastoral wisdom, he unlocks confusing and cliché concepts, and helps the average person to see how rich and necessary Leviticus is for Christian life and theology. I especially appreciated how effortlessly Scarlata shows how the New Testament weaves Jesus' teaching with Leviticus, then connects both to ordinary life today!"

—Dru Johnson, The King's College

A Journey through the World of Leviticus

A Journey through the World of Leviticus

Holiness, Sacrifice, and the Rock Badger

MARK W. SCARLATA

CASCADE Books • Eugene, Oregon

A JOURNEY THROUGH THE WORLD OF LEVITICUS
Holiness, Sacrifice, and the Rock Badger

Copyright © 2021 Mark W. Scarlata. All rights reserved. Except for brief quotations in critical publications or reviews, no part of this book may be reproduced in any manner without prior written permission from the publisher. Write: Permissions, Wipf and Stock Publishers, 199 W. 8th Ave., Suite 3, Eugene, OR 97401.

Cascade Books
An Imprint of Wipf and Stock Publishers
199 W. 8th Ave., Suite 3
Eugene, OR 97401

www.wipfandstock.com

PAPERBACK ISBN: 978-1-6667-1372-5
HARDCOVER ISBN: 978-1-6667-1373-2
EBOOK ISBN: 978-1-6667-1374-9

Cataloguing-in-Publication data:

Names: Scarlata, Mark William [author]

Title: A journey through the world of Leviticus : holiness, sacrifice, and the rock badger / Mark W. Scarlata.

Description: Eugene, OR: Cascade Books, 2021 | Includes bibliographical references and index.

Identifiers: ISBN 978-1-6667-1372-5 (paperback) | ISBN 978-1-6667-1373-2 (hardcover) | ISBN 978-1-6667-1374-9 (ebook)

Subjects: LCSH: Bible.—Leviticus—Introductions | Bible.—Leviticus—Study and teaching | Bible.—Leviticus—Criticism, interpretation, etc. | Holiness—Biblical teaching | Bible.—Pentateuch—Criticism, interpretation, etc.

Classification: BS1255.55 S33 2021 (paperback) | BS1255.5 (ebook)

11/12/21

Unless otherwise noted, all Scripture quotations are cited from the New Revised Standard Version, copyright © 1989 National Council of the Churches of Christ in the United States of America. Used by permission. All rights reserved worldwide.

For Bettina, Nathaniel, Madeleine, and Annabelle

Contents

Preface		xi
Acknowledgments		xv
1	The Sacred World *Looking through the Lens of Holiness*	1
2	Too Much Blood *Understanding Sacrifice and Atonement*	19
3	Nuclear Power, Alien Fire, and God's Home on Earth	38
4	You Are What You Eat *Food, Faithfulness, and Family*	59
5	Living in Holy Time *Finding God's Rhythm*	75
6	Purity, Pandemics, and Purification	94
7	Love Your Neighbor *Holiness, Empathy, and Artificial Intelligence*	113
For Reflection or Discussion		135
Works Cited		139
Scripture Index		141

Rock Badger or Rock Hyrax (*Procavia capensis*)

Preface

If you know anything about Leviticus, you might have guessed that this book would look at the themes of holiness and sacrifice. So why include the rock badger in the title? This little-known mammal, also called a hyrax, looks a bit like a gopher and makes its home in the rocks of the dry, Middle Eastern landscape. It only weighs around four kilograms (nine pounds) and makes loud grunting sounds while eating. Rock badgers are very social animals and form balanced, equal relationships among group members, which helps them survive longer. In an obscure command given in Leviticus 11:5 the Israelites are prohibited from eating this small creature because it's classed among other animals that "chew the cud," or ruminants, but do not have a cloven hoof. Interestingly, the rock badger does not chew the cud but may give the appearance of doing so when it eats. So why all this about rock badgers?

It's one of these quirky aspects of Leviticus that, on the surface, makes no sense at all to us modern readers but likely made perfect sense to its original audience. What does prohibiting the killing and consuming of a hyrax have to do with holiness? What's so important about not eating this sociable little creature in order to preserve the purity of God's people? Most commentators can only guess at possible answers and so we're left scratching our heads as to how this animal made it on the list of unclean things for Israel to eat. Yet it's these types of commands in Leviticus that demand our further attention because below the surface there is a deeper meaning for us to discover.

The point is that there are many aspects of Leviticus that contemporary readers find difficult to understand (especially a command about rock badgers!), which is why it's often one of the least read books of the Bible. Rather than digging into ancient Israelite culture, its symbols and their meaning, most people are more content to move on to other books of the Bible that are easier to digest. But this is where we lose out on the richness and depth of one of the most important books in the Old Testament.

Leviticus is not just a curious oddity with strange practices that have nothing to do with us. Leviticus is both a priestly and prophetic book that summarizes the entirety of God's commands for life and the centrality of the sacrificial system. Leviticus uses archetypal symbols, sounds, smells, and sights to help our imaginations come alive when we ponder the holiness and purity of God. It also offers ethical commands to care for the poor and the vulnerable, to live in justice and mercy, and to love your neighbor as yourself. Leviticus presents the fullness of God's instructions as they relate to every aspect of Israel's life so that they might become holy even as he is holy.

For all its strangeness and complexity, Leviticus has a very simple message—*pursue holiness in every part of your life so that you might become holy as God is holy* (Lev 19:2). God provides the only path that can lead to human flourishing, but it's a path that requires his people to submit every aspect of their lives to him. Whether it's eating, offering sacrifice, sexual relations, resting on the sabbath, or loving your neighbor as yourself, everything we do must be consecrated, set apart, and offered to him.

Why must we be holy? In the context of Leviticus, purity relates to the holy God who has descended from the heavens to inhabit his tabernacle on earth. His holiness now abides in the midst of his people and to remain in relationship with him one must be holy. The call to holiness, however, is not just central to Leviticus, it also applies to Christians who now have access to the indwelling Holy Spirit and can live in union with the Father through the Son. The command to live in holiness does not change from Old Testament to New Testament but, rather, it becomes possible through the life, death, resurrection, and ascension of the Son.

As you approach the book of Leviticus it will often feel like you've entered a strange new land where cultural traditions, rituals, and beliefs are dramatically different from our own. If you've ever travelled to a foreign country where you don't speak the language, you'll know that sense of unease you feel when you can't communicate with others or struggle to read the signs. Ordering a meal or getting directions becomes a major production and can often lead to frustration and despair. But if you stay in that country for some time and begin to understand the language and the cultural traditions of its people, a greater appreciation and understanding opens up. This is what it's like when we begin to grasp the world of Leviticus.

This book is somewhat like a theological travel log to help the traveler through this strange new world. The hope is that with a little insight into this ancient culture and its practices, one can come to a greater appreciation for how God instructed his people through ritual, signs, and symbols and how these are further revealed in Christ. My hope is that by exploring the riches of Leviticus, the profound mystery of the gospel of Christ will be unveiled even further. But to grasp these connections between Leviticus and the New Testament takes some work. It may seem like a struggle at times, but it's a worthy struggle if it reveals more of the beauty of the Son and a vision for our personal and corporate call to holiness in him.

I have not included excessive footnotes in this theological travel log, but the influence of scholarly wisdom can be found throughout these pages. I am particularly indebted to the work of Jacob Milgrom, Baruch Levine, Mary Douglas, Gary Anderson, Samuel Balentine, Gordon Wenham, Catherine Bell, and others who have been so influential in my understanding of Leviticus.

With these things in mind, lets buckle up and make our way into a new land to discover God's chosen people, the ancient Israelites, who were called to holiness and to be a witness of his glory in the world. And as we do, may we also remember the Christian call to holiness in Christ to bring his wholeness, healing, and life into the world.

Acknowledgments

It always seems an impossible task to acknowledge all those who have helped in the shaping of any book. Like most of my writing, it was born out of engagement with my students and my teaching in the wider church. This particular work on Leviticus was largely the product of the pandemic lockdowns where most of us were forced out of our churches and classrooms and into the digital realms. It began with a four-week course through the St. Paul's Theological Centre's "School of Theology," where an eager group of lay people had the patience to suffer through my ramblings about the beauty of Leviticus, the sacred world, and our call to holiness. Their questions and comments were an inspiration and reminded me that *all* Scripture is critical in the formation of our life and faith—even Leviticus! These ideas were then brought into the classrooms of St. Mellitus College, where my students pushed and challenged my readings of Leviticus and in so doing opened up more ideas on how this ancient text can speak to our modern world. Further discussions were had with many of our PhD scholars at the St. Edward's Scriptorium who, again, had the patience to put up with my constantly drawing all things back to Leviticus. This group is committed to the highest level of Christian scholarship and to the corporate life of prayer and I found it a great support through the darker times of lockdown.

I'm grateful for those who took the time to read early versions of the book and for their comments; Chris Scarlata, Matthew Johnson, Peter Elliott, and Dru Johnson. I'm also thankful for the support of my students and colleagues at St. Mellitus as well as those in my parish of St. Edward's, Cambridge. Thanks also to Cascade Books editor Robin Parry and his support for a lay book on Leviticus. Other publishers balked at the idea that Leviticus could sell, so I'm grateful to the Cascade imprint for being willing to take a risk. Most of all I'm thankful for the support of my wife, Bettina, and our children Nathaniel, Madeleine, and Annabelle, who have taught me most about what it means to grow in holiness as a family.

St. Edward, King and Martyr, Cambridge 2021

1

The Sacred World

Looking through the Lens of Holiness

THE SACRED WORLD

To begin our journey we'll want to orientate ourselves to the lay of the land. The first step will be to understand what life was like in ancient Israel and how the people understood God's presence in the world. This is important, especially when we consider how a modern, secular society has all but lost any sense of the sacred. Next, we'll see how Leviticus fits within the biblical narrative of the Old Testament and why it's so concerned with things like purity and sacrifice. Then we'll look at Leviticus in relation to the creation story of Genesis 1, which will help make sense of why there's so much emphasis on dividing and keeping things in their proper categories. Finally, we'll explore the concept of holiness and how it was understood in Leviticus and how it relates to Christians today.

It's difficult to imagine what life was like for the Israelites and their surrounding neighbors in the ancient Near East. Unlike our rational and scientific approach to life, most ancient cultures believed that the world was filled with malevolent powers and that life was governed by the gods. These gods didn't care much for humanity. They were often capricious and largely indifferent to human suffering. Today we might take out insurance policies or plan strategic investments to secure our future, but the ancients went down to their local altars to give offerings or slaughter animals so that the gods might look favorably upon them. Maybe they would provide rain for their crops so that they could feed their family. One could only hope that the gods were listening as people went about their daily lives trying to survive.

Life in ancient, self-sustaining farming communities was unpredictable and often teetered on the verge of catastrophe. What do you do if there's no rain or if a stronger tribe attacks your village? Where do you go if there's no food in a prolonged drought? There were no pensions or financial security, no concept of retirement and taking it easy. Life was lived day to day, season to season, according to the cycles of seedtime and harvest. Everyone worked to ensure the survival of the family and the future of the next generation.

How drastically different our understanding of the world is today! A secular society has little room for divine activity in daily life. Rain doesn't come from the gods, but it can be predicted by studying weather patterns and using advanced supercomputers. Disease is not a sign of divine anger, but it's the natural result of bacteria or genetic disorders that we trust can be overcome through advances in medicine. Fertility is no longer a sign of divine blessing, but it can be achieved through artificial insemination or genetic modification. The food that most people eat is not the product of small, local farms but comes from industrial-scale agribusiness. The animals we eat are no longer a part of our family ecosystem but are treated like products for consumption as they are grown (often with artificial hormones or other drugs) solely for the purpose of being slaughtered, packaged, and shipped throughout the world. In a modern industrialized society science and technology have replaced the gods and have offered hope through the power of human ingenuity to provide for our every need.

One of the results of our Western secular and technology-driven society is that we have little understanding of the world as a sacred place inhabited by the divine. We have done away with any concept of spiritual influence and have made ourselves the sole champions of our destinies. We have no need of the miraculous when we can trust in scientific explanation. We have no use for prayer because we can build machines or manufacture drugs to satisfy our needs. We have no use for God because we trust that technology and human knowledge will ultimately provide solutions to all our problems.

The world we live in today is one that has been *desacralized*. We no longer witness God's presence in the places we inhabit, the people we meet, or in our encounters with creation. We fail to perceive his glory as it is revealed before us in both the spectacular and the mundane. The world has become disenchanted and the result is that our perception of the sacred has been diminished. We rely so much on our rational, cognitive abilities that even worship in our churches can become a functional event rather than a mystical encounter with the divine.

David Brown speaks about how we have lost the "enchantment of place" in the modern world. He writes that the dominant way of thinking today suggests that once we can explain something there is no further need to address religious questions.[1] So, for example, if we understand the genetic composition of a seed and the process of photosynthesis, then we no longer stand in awe of the growth of a plant. Or if we can see inside the womb and calculate each stage of a fetus' development, then we no longer consider birth a miraculous event. The moment that we can explain something scientifically is the moment that we feel like we have lifted some mysterious veil and, consequently, no longer see the need for God.

This is not to say that there's anything wrong with scientific progress or the advances in technology that have helped us understand our world. The sciences have opened up amazing mysteries that previous generations could not have dreamed of and there are many more that science has yet to discover. What is needed, however, is a re-balancing between the rational and the sacred. What is needed is an understanding that scientific explanations do not replace God but can draw us further into the wonder and mystery of his presence around us. What is needed is the *re-sacralization* of the world.

To rediscover the sacred around us means that we hold together both our spiritual experience and our rational thought in order to discern the truth. Oftentimes we may want to rationalize or explain every experience, but this may reduce an encounter to a logical chain of events without acknowledging God's presence in those events. There's nothing wrong with examining the world through a scientific lens or using our rational capacities, but if this is the *only* way we perceive reality then we might be missing how God is moving in our midst. When we begin to see God's presence in all things, we discover how we fit within the vast, complex, and interconnected web of life where his holiness emanates around us in every moment and in every place.

Think about those times when we witness something in the world that might draw us back to its sacredness. It might be a stunning sunrise or sunset, or a rainbow in the sky after a storm. In that moment we might feel God's presence, we might witness the beauty of his creation and possibly meditate on our own insignificance within the universe. Our scientific knowledge of how a rainbow is created through the refraction of light, or

---

1. Brown, *God and Enchantment of Space*, 22.

our understanding of the many neural synapses going on in our brains, may enhance our experience but we don't stop with our analysis of the physical world. Instead, we allow the physical experience to lead us to the spiritual realities that help us witness the glory of God's kingdom in our midst.

Imagine what it would be like if we were wholly attuned to God's abiding presence in the world? What would it feel like if we lived with the understanding that everything in creation, down to its subatomic particles, was radiating with God's glory? And how would we respond if we perceived that glory in every human being created in God's image?

The book of Leviticus invites us to explore such a world. It beckons us to experience a life where the holy God, the creator of the heavens and the earth, has come down and moved into the neighborhood. Imagine if God lived a few doors down from you. Imagine if when you walked out your door in the morning you could see his glory beaming through the windows. Imagine that the further you got away from his home the more you began to notice his presence in the trees, the birds, the squirrel that runs across the street. And imagine if you began to see his face reflected in the face of your neighbor and in the face of every human being. This is the world of Leviticus, where God's holiness is present in his home, the tabernacle. This small tent that Israel was commanded to make in Exodus is designed with materials and items that recall the garden of Eden, the place where God once dwelled with humanity. Detailed blueprints were given to Moses because the tabernacle not only represents Eden, but it also represents the entire cosmos.

We'll discuss the tabernacle and holy space in detail in chapter 3, but it's enough to say that its structure and design represent a microcosm of the heavens and the earth. God dwells in the holy of holies in the innermost sanctum and his glory radiates outward like concentric circles rippling through all creation. But if the tabernacle contains God's holiness, how can an unclean, unholy people live in his presence? This is the fundamental concern of Leviticus and its understanding of the sacred world.

Sadly, the book of Leviticus has often been characterized by both Jews and Christians as strange, impenetrable, and more concerned with the blood of animals than the flourishing of humanity. Some see it as a book about religious regulations, stringent rules around sacrifice, and priests who lock themselves away behind temple walls completely separated from the people.

Reading Leviticus from this perspective potentially turns God into some sort of rigid school master. He stands ready to strike a child on the wrist with a ruler if they commit the most minor infraction, rather than the loving father who runs with opens arms to receive the prodigal son. Because of this, most Christians are happy to do away with Leviticus in the name of Jesus, who came to teach about love and grace. Yet, as we shall see, even Jesus upholds the teachings of Leviticus throughout his life and uses its commands and rituals to help define his gospel message.

The sacred world of Leviticus is one that is saturated in holiness. Holiness encompasses every aspect of life because God is holy and is wholly present in the world. His holiness does not merely require the proper butchering of an animal, but it's concerned with how we treat our neighbor, our family, foreign refugees, animals, and the land. All of life is wrapped in a beautiful web of holiness for Leviticus and all of life must be consecrated as holy if God's people are to remain in unity with him and in his presence.

There is a pressing need for the study of Leviticus in the church today and especially in a modern secular culture that has substituted rationality for religious experience. The diminishing of holiness and the desacralization of the world comes at a cost. Without acknowledging the immanence and transcendence of God in creation, life can be reduced to a series of propositional truths and empirical evidence that strip the world of its mystery and the presence of the divine. As Walter Brueggemann writes, "The holiness of God is urgent in the face of profanation, which empties life of larger passion and dignity. The holiness of God is urgent in the face of pervasive brutality, which trivializes God's purpose and abuses God's world. The holiness of God is urgent in the face of growing authority of technique, which diminishes mystery that keeps life open."[2] It's this urgency that compels us to read afresh the text of Leviticus, to comprehend the breadth of its teaching, and to witness its vision of God's holy and sacred world.

SETTING THE STAGE FOR THE BOOK OF LEVITICUS

To understand Leviticus we first need to set the scene for where the book is situated and how it fits within the larger story of the Bible. God's liberation of his people from Egypt stands as the most significant act of redemption in the Old Testament. Apart from Genesis, the entire Pentateuch (the first five books of the Bible) is concerned with God rescuing his children from bondage in Egypt so that they might live freely to worship him and to be his people in the land he had promised to Abraham.

Exodus begins in Egypt where the descendants of Abraham, Isaac, and Jacob have been enslaved by a brutal and merciless regime under the pharaohs. For four hundred years they suffered with no hope of freedom, despite the promise and covenant God made with Abraham centuries before.

2. Brueggemann, foreword to *Holiness in Israel*, xii.

God told Abraham that he would inherit a vast land and would have descendants that would be like the stars in the sky (Genesis 15). Those would have seemed like distant dreams compared to the harsh reality that the people faced under the iron fist of Pharaoh.

The main (human) character of the Pentateuch is Moses. He is called by God to deliver the Hebrew slaves from Egypt to the promised land, but this was no easy task. After a series of plagues and the parting of the sea, the dramatic exit from Egypt is orchestrated by God through his servant Moses. Israel spends forty years wandering through the Sinai Peninsula before they make their way to their new home. In the midst of this journey we encounter the great pause of the Pentateuch when Moses and the people reach Mt. Sinai to enter into covenant with God and to receive his teachings and commandments.

The instructions given to Moses are often referred to as the "law" of the Old Testament, but most of God's teaching looks far different from our notion of law today. Take, for example, the tenth commandment, "You shall not covet." Coveting is something that happens within a person's heart and mind and would be virtually impossible to convict someone of in a court of law. Coveting, however, when it grows into full-blown sin, can result in theft or something worse. The more that I covet what others have—be it money, fame, possessions, power, health, or good looks—the less satisfied I am with my own life and the less grateful I become for what I do have. Coveting can lead to a vicious spiral of ungratefulness, envy, uncontrolled jealousy, and sin against our neighbor if we're not careful. But the command is not so much a law as we might think of it being enforced by a judge. It's an instruction that's meant to lead to the wholeness and flourishing of the individual, the family, and the community of faith.

Moses also receives God's commandments on how to build the tabernacle so that Israel might worship him as his chosen people. In Exodus one of the most monumental changes in history was not just that God delivered his people, but that he wanted to come down from the heavens to abide permanently among them. God says to Moses, "Let them build me a tabernacle that I may dwell in their midst" (Exod 25:4). The great story of salvation in the Old Testament is not just about being liberated from death and slavery, it's also about *relationship*—the relationship that God wants to have with his people by living in the heart of their community.

By the end of Exodus the building of the tabernacle is complete and God's glory comes down and fills the space with such power, radiance, and holiness that not even Moses can enter (Exodus 40). And it's here that we find our bridge to Leviticus. If God is so holy that no one can approach him, how can God's people worship him and draw near to him? This is where the instructions and teaching of Leviticus come in and set out to answer the question of how unholy people can live in the presence of a holy God.

This is where we need to pause for a moment and think about the *particularity* of the book of Leviticus and why it's so concerned with purity, holiness, and sacrifice. God's rules were not intended to micromanage everything his people did in his presence. Instead, his commandments offer an overarching framework for how an unclean people can be purified so that they might draw near to his holiness and remain in relationship with him.

To draw near to God, however, required both ritual and ethical purity. This meant that you needed to make sacrifices, perform ritual washings, and eat certain foods. But it also meant that you needed to treat others with justice and mercy. Both ritual acts and moral living were critical to preserving the holiness of God's sanctuary. One could not be separated from the other. To ensure God's holiness remained present in the tabernacle, Israel needed to perform the rituals God instituted and to live together as a people governed by his justice, righteousness, and grace.

In some ways we might think of Leviticus as setting the stage for a new world order. Never before since the days of Eden had God dwelt with humanity on earth. But now this holy God is coming back to inaugurate a new creation, a new Eden, by making his home in the midst of his people. He has come to bless them, and the world, with his presence. Leviticus marks the dawn of a new age for Israel and for all nations. God has come down from heaven to dwell with his people, to bring them his salvation, and to teach them about how to live in his holy presence. This is why Leviticus is so concerned with holiness.

The other point about the *particularity* of Leviticus is that these instructions for holiness were written to a group of subsistence farmers and shepherds who lived in small clans and tribal settlements in the Middle East over three thousand years ago. That's slightly different than modern day London or New York! So we have to be careful not to fall into the trap of literalism, which is a trap for both Christians and those cynics and skeptics of the Bible.

Some Christians have used Leviticus to condemn homosexual behavior by citing certain laws (Lev 18:22), but they happily skim over other laws that permit slaves and polygamy. The problem is that we cannot pick and choose which commands we prefer because the whole of the law was intended to lead to holiness and not just isolated parts of it.

Cynics, on the other hand, will take passages like Lev 12:2, which refers to a woman's ritual uncleanness during menstruation, and mock the idea that women in the modern world should be considered impure because of natural bodily functions. They denounce the Bible as sexist, antiquated, and useless for the modern, enlightened human being.

Both of these approaches, however, misuse and misunderstand the text of Leviticus. Anyone can take a biblical passage out of its context and twist it to support their own beliefs or use it to demonstrate how worthless religion is to contemporary society. These approaches are especially dangerous in the case of Leviticus if we don't understand it within the context of the ancient world in which it was written.

The challenge we have is determining how a religious text written thousands of years ago can speak to us today. One possible approach is to interpret the commandments in Leviticus by analogy. The more we can learn more about the cultural background of ancient Israel, the more we understand what the text might have meant to those in the ancient world. This may not work for every Old Testament command, but it allows us to look for the principle behind God's word so that we might use that by analogy today.[3]

Take, for example, Lev 19:9–10: "When you reap the harvest of your land, you shall not reap to the very edges of your field, or gather the gleanings of your harvest. You shall not strip your vineyard bare, or gather the fallen grapes of your vineyard; you shall leave them for the poor and the alien: I am the LORD your God." If we interpreted this literally it wouldn't make much sense today since a majority of the poor and those in need are found in urban centers and cities throughout the world. It's also clear that this command wasn't written with combine harvesters or industrial-scale farming in mind.

The command was written to small clans of ancient Israelites who practiced subsistence farming, which meant that they often produced just enough for their own family. Living as a farmer in Israel was fraught with anxieties about having enough food to put on the table or having enough seed for the next planting season. To ask God for one's "daily bread" was to trust that he would provide rain, protect crops from blight or drought, and give fertility to livestock and the fields. With this in mind, let's go back to God's teaching. To leave the edges of one's field unharvested was not just giving to the poor out of one's abundance. It was a real sacrifice out of what the family needed to survive.

If we take the command and apply it by analogy to today's world we see that God's desire is for us to give sacrificially from what we produce by our work (in the New Testament this often amounts to selling everything and giving to the poor). Most of us aren't harvesting fields, but that

---

3. See Wright, *Old Testament Ethics*, 321–24.

doesn't mean we can't give out of what we do. This may be giving to those in need through financial means, it might be offering our time, our service, or something that relates to our trade. The artist might give from their creative works. The musician might bless others with their gifts. The plumber might offer their services. Whatever the profession, we all have *something* we can give sacrificially to bless those around us in need. I was recently reminded of an orthodontist who offered free dental care through her practice to those who couldn't afford it. This is one of the ways that God wants us to be a holy people by caring for the poor out of the gifts he has given to us.

What we also see in the command is the dignity that people are afforded when they're able to work. Gleaning the fields was no easy task and took physical effort and time. We see this in the book of Ruth when she and Naomi return to Bethlehem to glean the edges of Boaz's fields. Though the owner of the field is offering a gift from their produce, those who receive it must also work for it. If we apply that principal today we might think of those in need of work. Leaving the edges of our fields might also mean creating opportunities for employment for those who are struggling to find dignity in an honest job.

When we discover the principles of faith behind the instructions in Leviticus we can, in some instances, find parallels or analogies with our contemporary world. This is, in fact, what Paul did with the Old Testament when teaching new followers of Christ. In speaking about the wages that should come to those whose livelihood was to proclaim the gospel, Paul says that you shouldn't muzzle an ox while it's treading out the grain, quoting from Deuteronomy 25. Paul takes the Old Testament concept of letting an animal eat while it works and applies it to his current status as an apostle of Christ and says that the command was actually written for his situation (1 Cor 9:10–12). Paul sees the Old Testament teaching on the humane care of farm animals as analogous to those apostles traveling around the Roman world to proclaim the gospel of Christ.

To understand Leviticus, then, we must transport ourselves back to an ancient and foreign world where "law" is something different than what we might think it is. In the wilderness of Sinai God gave his people instructions on how to live in holiness. His teaching was not a burden to his people, nor was it given to weigh them down with unnecessary rituals and religious regulations. Instead, his commands were a gift and Israel's obedience was their appropriate and grateful response to that gift. The teaching revealed in Leviticus was a sign of grace that came from the God who delivered his people from death and promised to plant them in their own land so that they might thrive and grow as a holy people to bring life to the world.

LEVITICUS AND CREATION

The call to holiness is central to Leviticus, but that call is also framed within the order of God's creation. To understand how these things fit together we need to take one giant step back as we survey the land and the sacred world of Leviticus. We need to look to the patterns God establishes in creation if we are to discover the patterns and symbols that Leviticus uses as a framework for holiness. If the creation of the world was the result of God's wisdom in ordering and dividing all things, then Leviticus seeks to reflect that same order and division in the life of God's people.

When we go back to the creation story of Genesis 1:1—2:3 we find that there are distinct differences from the more earthy creation story of Genesis 2. In the first account, God brings order out of chaos when all that existed was "formless and void" (Gen 1:2). The universe was a big cosmic mess of material that had yet to be shaped into something of beauty by the spoken word of God. Unlike the gardener God of Genesis 2, who gets his hands dirty in the soil of the earth and fashions humanity like a potter, the God of Genesis 1 is in the heavens and brings forth life through the utterance of his word. By divine command the material world takes shape, it is blessed, and it is good.

A verb frequently used throughout Leviticus is "divide" (*hivdil* in Hebrew). We find this same verb used in the beginning of Genesis. "And God saw that the light was good, and God *divided* the light from the darkness. . . . And God made the dome and it *divided* the waters beneath the dome from the waters above the dome, and it was so" (Gen 1:3, 7, my translation). This vision of creation is one in which life emerges from chaos by the proper ordering of disparate elements. God's order and division prevents the world from spiraling back into chaos and offers a framework for the fertility and blessing of all life.

Though the word "division" often takes on negative connotations, we might think of the original creation like one big messy blob of paint where all the colors have been mixed together. For the artist to be able to use the paints, they must first be divided into their separate categories and placed in their pots. Once the paints are separated, then the artist can begin to use them. This is like the type of division we see happening in the beginning. It's as if God, the great artist, is setting his paints in their proper place so that the creation may begin to take its shape as a living, breathing work of art.

In some ways, Genesis 1 might be considered the first story of salvation in the Bible, as the material world moves from chaos to order. This is an important concept for the priests of ancient Israel. Proper division and separation are pathways to blessing. God divides all creatures and plants according to their kind. The water is filled with fish and teeming with living creatures while the air is filled with birds. The land produces trees with fruit and seed-bearing vegetation along with animals who reproduce according to their kind. Humanity is created in the image of God with a special mandate not only to "be fruitful and multiply" but to watch over and to care for God's creation. Each separation and categorization represent a movement in the salvation of the physical world.

When all the divisions in the material world are complete and everything that God made was "very good," he separates one more thing by consecrating Sabbath time. Genesis 2:3 says that God blessed the seventh day and "hallowed it," or made it holy, and divided it from normal time. We'll discuss later how critical the Sabbath is for Leviticus, but for the moment it's enough to remember that the movement of God's creation ends in wholeness and rest. Time becomes holy as it is sanctified by God and will be a sign for Israel as they too are called to follow his pattern of work and rest.

What the creation story of Genesis 1 reveals is a God who blesses through order and who, in his wisdom, creates natural boundaries between plants, animals, humans, and the whole of creation. Each part of the world plays its role in bringing forth God's blessing by doing what it was created to do. The complexity and interdependence of all things relies on maintaining God's classifications and divisions. The sea needs to stay in its appointed place. The sun and moon need to travel consistently across the sky to mark times and seasons. The animals and other creatures need to reproduce with their own kind. Human beings need to reflect God's image as they care for the world. When all things act according to God's design the world will be fruitful, life-giving, and very good.

Consequently, if the boundaries that God has set are crossed it leads to disorder and ultimately a return to chaos. This is what we find when humanity departs from Eden. In Genesis 4, Cain murders his brother Abel. We then follow a dramatic decline to Genesis 6 where we learn that all humanity has become utterly corrupt, except for Noah. This leads to the flood and the destruction all of creation. When God's world is profaned by sin it moves back toward a state of chaos and it is only by his grace that humanity and creation are given a second chance.

The balance between order and chaos is critical for Leviticus. This same process of "dividing" is repeated throughout the book, whether it's how you sacrifice an animal and divide its parts, how you divide food into what you can and cannot eat, how you deal with disease, or even sexual matters. The process of ordering and dividing is seen in Leviticus as a sacred act that preserves God's natural order in creation. And the priests are commissioned with the task of making sure this happens. "You are to *divide* between the holy and the common, and between the unclean and the clean; and you are to teach the people of Israel all the statutes that the LORD has spoken to them through Moses" (Lev 10:10–11, my translation).

In Leviticus, the sacred world is a world that is ordered according to God's wisdom. The key for God's people is to maintain that order so that boundaries are not crossed and so that all of Israel learns the difference between things that are consecrated as holy and things that are profane.

It's also important when reading Leviticus that we understand some of the terms that it uses to describe these divisions. We might think of the word "profane" as a reference to something that is evil or bad. To call something profane in Leviticus does not necessarily mean that it's bad, but it refers to the state of something in relation to God's dwelling place. The English word "profane" comes from the Latin roots *pro-* ("before") and *fanum* ("temple"), which refers to those things that are literally before the temple, or outside the temple. The profane is that which exists in the ordinary, everyday world rather than inside the holy place of God. Things that are profane have not been consecrated or set aside for holy purposes, but this does not mean that they are somehow "bad."

Ultimately all things are consecrated as holy through Christ, but in Leviticus there is a very clear distinction between the state of people or things in the ordinary, profane world and those things that have been set apart to be near God's presence in the tabernacle. So what is profane in Leviticus is not necessarily bad but, rather, it refers to *a state of being unconsecrated and remaining outside the temple.*

One last thing to say about some of the terms that Leviticus uses to describe the categories of God's creation. The words "holy" and "profane," "clean" and "unclean," "pure" and "impure" all represent *ritual states of being in relationship to the tabernacle that can change over time.* Some animals or creatures are always unclean for Israel, but people move from states of purity to impurity as a natural part of life. Sometimes this is the result of sin, but other times it's simply the result of who we are as human beings.

For example, women are considered ritually unclean after childbirth (Leviticus 12). For a certain period they need to stay away from the tabernacle because they have brought life into the world. If God commanded humans to be fruitful and multiply (Gen 1:28) why would he then exclude women from approaching his presence after giving birth and fulfilling his command? The point is not that the woman has sinned, but that her body is in a state of purification after childbirth as it continues to release blood and so it is ritually unclean. This rule may have been enforced to protect women or it may have had to do with an ancient understanding of the power of blood. Whatever the reason, it's important to remember that when something is unclean or profane in Leviticus it does *not* mean that it's sinful or evil. *Ritual impurity does not always imply moral impurity.*

Understanding the natural order of creation will help us understand some aspects of how and why God prescribes certain things for his people. It won't answer every question, but it will help us make sense of how the ancient Israelites viewed their world. Separation, classification, interdependence, unity in diversity, harmony—all of these terms capture the way Leviticus sees God's wisdom expressed in creation and how they should reflect that wisdom in living as a holy people.

THE CALL TO HOLINESS

The book of Leviticus is fundamentally concerned about holiness because God is holy and he calls his people to be holy. Too often, however, the images that people conjure up when thinking about holiness are of those who elevate or separate themselves from others. We might think of some priest or self-righteous churchgoer donning spotless clothes and sneering at anyone with questionable morals. They distance themselves from the riff-raff of the world and keep company with other upright people like themselves. Their goal is to remain unstained by the dirt and filth of the world around them so that they might remain pure and pristine. Normal people get dirty in everyday life, but not those who are holy. How perfectly this is summed up by the Pharisee in Jesus' parable who prays, "God, I thank you that I am not like other people: thieves, rogues, adulterers, or even like this tax collector" (Luke 18:11).

The trouble with this kind of image is that it does not express the holiness God prescribes in Leviticus or the holiness we see in Christ. Instead, it reflects a perversion of holiness that turns inward on itself rather than outward toward others. This results in whitewashed exteriors that look righteous on the outside but are rotting away on the inside. So often the pursuit of holiness can be twisted by our egos and it can become a path that isolates us from those whom we are called to love. Whether this is done individually or collectively, it can lead to factions and tribalism that reject the other because they are unholy, or not a part of the chosen group.

This ego-driven holiness is what we see portrayed in the New Testament through depictions of some Jewish religious leaders. In their desire for holiness they had mistakenly separated themselves from others by being content in their own moral and cultic purity. They looked down on others like tax collectors or sinners because they didn't live up to the same standards of purity that they had achieved. By no means were all the Pharisees or religious Jews of Jesus' day like this, but there were some who thought of themselves as so clean, so righteous, and so pure that they could not bear to interact with the dregs of society or the unclean of the world. Sadly, similar attitudes can be found among many Christians today.

Part of the problem lies in how we understand the New Testament idea of pursuing holiness rather than worldliness. The rejection of the "world" is often misunderstood as a rejection of people, culture, society, and even creation. Christians often divide the world into what is good (spiritual) and what is bad (material or "flesh") without recognizing that both physical and spiritual things are part of God's creation, which is being reconciled in Christ.

The New Testament call to holiness and a rejection of the "world" is not to turn away from others or our physical surroundings, but it's to reject the perverted ways of humanity that end in abuse, manipulation, violence, and death. To cast off the "world" is also to turn from our own inner corruption so that we might engage with society and culture to bring about healing, reconciliation, and the goodness of God's kingdom here on earth. Holiness in the New Testament is concerned with the redemption of both the physical and the spiritual through the Holy Spirit and the work of Christ.

To better understand the biblical idea of holiness it may be helpful to go back to how the concept was understood in the Old Testament. The Hebrew word for holiness (*kodesh*) has the sense of something that is *set apart*. God is the source of all holiness and things that are set apart to him become holy. This could refer to material things, like the tools used for worship, or it could refer to people, like the priests working in the tabernacle. When something was washed, consecrated, and set apart to God as holy it somehow acquired a measure of his holiness.

The process of setting things apart for holy purposes was not reserved for priests or those things that were associated with the tabernacle. God calls for all of his people to pursue the highest level of holiness. "Speak to all the congregation of the people of Israel and say to them: You shall be holy, for I the LORD your God am holy" (Lev 19:2). To be set apart as a holy people means that everyone must strive to reflect God's love, compassion, mercy, and justice. When this happens, holiness becomes a collective sign of God's blessing upon his people and a witness to the nations.

Israel did not immediately become holy when they were set apart by God to be his people. Holiness came through life-long obedience to his commands. This required repentance, sacrifice for sin, reconciliation with one's neighbor, appropriate treatment of the land, performing rituals, caring for those in need, and even eating the right foods. Holiness was never a static concept but required the re-consecration of every aspect of one's life each day. Covenant obedience, or discipleship, was a whole life commitment and required the people to examine themselves in the light of God's holiness and his presence in the tabernacle.

For the Christian, growing in holiness is also a daily re-consecration of life as we set ourselves apart to Christ and are incorporated into his body. Holiness is not something we acquire once and then desperately try to cling to. It's a process of turning away from our old selves and being renewed and transformed by God's love. The more our hearts are purified, the more they reflect Christ's holiness and the more we begin to experience God's sacred presence in the world. Thomas Merton writes, "The true saint is not one who has become convinced that he himself is holy, but one who is overwhelmed by the realization that God, and God alone, is holy. He is so awestruck with the reality of the divine holiness that he begins to see it everywhere."[4]

The pursuit of holiness is a wholistic process that requires the submission of every aspect of our lives, whether it's in what we eat or drink, what we buy, how we treat others, or how we pray and study the Scripture. When we commit the entirety of both our physical and spiritual lives to God, we draw nearer to him and in doing so, we draw nearer to those around us. As we experience God's holiness, the more we are compelled by his love for humanity. And the more our hearts are compelled by his love, the more we will want to show his compassion and mercy to all people, especially the poor, the oppressed, or the alien among us. Union with God's holiness always leads to union with those created in his image.

Israel was called to be a holy people in Leviticus because God wanted to set them apart from the perversions of the world so that they would draw near to him and become a people who fully embraced his world in love. The tragedy we see throughout the Old Testament, and in the church today, is the self-centered response of those who perceive holiness as isolation, rejection of the other, and the preservation of the chosen few.

Though there are often stereotypes of the God of Leviticus as cold, aloof, legalistic, and only concerned with prescribed sacrifices, this is far from the picture we get in the book. The God revealed in Leviticus is the Holy Father who has redeemed his firstborn son, Israel, from slavery and death in Egypt to be set apart as a holy people (Exod 4:22–23). As Israel draws near to the heart of the Father, so too are they to express his love for the world. This is the holiness that we see in the life of Christ, the only begotten Son, who expressed his unity with the Father through his love toward those whom the Father loves.

The call to holiness in Leviticus is ultimately a call to relationship and to the Father's love. Though it was written to an ancient agrarian and pastoral

---

4. Merton, *Life and Holiness*, 26.

people in the Middle East traveling across the Sinai Peninsula, Leviticus draws us back to the call of holiness that sets us apart for the sake of expressing God's love for the world. Today this call remains the vocation of every Christian.

Israel's call to holiness, however, was not an individual calling but together they were to become a "kingdom of priests" and a "holy nation" (Exod 19:6). Likewise, Peter calls the new Christian community "a chosen race, a royal priesthood, a holy nation, God's own people" (1 Pet 2:9). Holiness is a *communal* endeavor. It requires the interdependence of people living together and expressing the love of Christ to one another. Holiness is not something that anyone can achieve on their own. The call to holiness is God's command to the *whole* covenant community and not just a select few. God redeems his people out of Egypt and they must walk *together* to the promised land.

This is an important point for our Western, highly individualized and self-centered consumer culture. We are mistaken if we think that personal piety and the compartmentalization of our spiritual lives can lead to holiness. As if we could just pull up our bootstraps and live a holy life on our own strength. Without being deeply immersed in the church, the new covenant community of faith, we risk becoming spiritual consumers seeking to satisfy our own personal desires or needs and not those of the other. Holy living requires mutual relationships of interdependence within the body of Christ.

Our experience thus far in the twenty-first century reminds us of the dangers of personal piety that lacks any social engagement or justice. Like the previous century, we have already witnessed political dictators in countries that have been traditionally called Christian. The blindness of some Christians to unjust structures, environmental destruction, racist institutions, and all other kinds of evil, demonstrates that claiming to have a personal, private faith is a pale veneer of religion that means nothing. Individual, self-centered piety is not holiness. It can lead to a spiritual narcissism that becomes consumed with the self and goes deaf to the cry of injustice and oppression that God is so quick to hear (cf. Exod 2:24).

To truly experience holiness is to experience God in and through others. This is at the heart of holiness in Leviticus and why the call to be holy as God is holy (Lev 19:2) sits right beside the parallel command to love your neighbor as yourself (Lev 19:18). Only in relationship with God and neighbor can holiness be fulfilled as the summary of the law.

This pursuit of holiness might seem to be a terrifying prospect. How can we ever expect to be holy as God is holy? For some this might seem too demanding a command and so, instead, they are satisfied with a little holiness, a little goodness, a little mercy. But Merton reminds us that, "if we are called by God to holiness of life, and if holiness is beyond our natural power to achieve (which it certainly is) then it follows that God himself must give us the light, the strength, and the courage to fulfill the task he requires of us."[5] Holiness is not something we achieve by our own strength. It comes through submission to the Holy Spirit in Christ. The more we give up our old selves, our pride, our independence, and our strength, the more Christ comes within to purify us in his holiness.

As we are purified, we grow in our understanding of our connection to the body of Christ and to the holiness of the church. We begin to realize that it is through our brothers and sisters in Christ that we are upheld, spurred on, and driven toward holiness. Christ did not leave us alone to fulfill his commands, but he joined us together in the power of the Spirit to become his holy temple on earth.

God's command to be holy as he is holy is not designed to set us up for failure. Instead, the call to holiness is one that encourages us to believe in the possibility that we *can* change. There is no need to live with small ambitions or be satisfied with mediocrity in the life of faith because God has given us all that we need to become holy. In Leviticus this came in the form of God's command through Moses. In the New Testament it comes through the promise of the indwelling Spirit so that the words of Jeremiah might be fulfilled, "I will put my law within them, and I will write it on their hearts; and I will be their God, and they shall be my people" (Jer 31:33). The goodness and challenge of the command no longer brings fear but becomes a joyful work of love from the heart.

When God's command is written on our heart we begin to understand the desires of his holiness. Jesus criticized the Pharisees for being hypocritical in their outward demonstrations of piety that lacked an inner love and mercy toward others (Matthew 23). The problem wasn't that the Pharisees weren't following the commands in Leviticus regarding holiness. The issue was that they had lost sight of the more significant commands regarding justice and mercy and so Jesus says to them, "You neglect the weightier matters of the law" (Matt 23:23).

The laws in Leviticus came from the very mouth of God through Moses and were not deficient in any way, but like any command they could be twisted and manipulated to become empty of its original intent. The Pharisees had substituted the inner life of mercy and charity for the outward scaffolding of ritual obedience. Both, however, were needed. The commands of God offered a framework for how to be holy, but they were always meant to be lived under the weighty summary of the law—to love God and to love your neighbor as yourself.

5. Merton, *Holiness*, 17.

Holiness is about getting dirty in the profound depths of unity and love that we discover in God and in our relationships with others. Holiness is God's desire for every person to be transformed from the old into the new. True holiness is not stale, austere, or removed from the trials, pains, and joys of everyday life. Holiness is the purity and wholeness of God's love made know through each one when we are united with him in Christ.

Holiness is also something that takes time. We continue to grow and change from day to day when we pursue love and purity in every aspect of our lives. One does not become holy and then simply remain holy by trying not to sin. Holiness is always a movement toward God through Christ that requires a constant striving in the life of faith.

If we fail, sin, fall short, become impure, we do not instantly become unholy. What Leviticus stresses, and what the New Testament authors also emphasize, is the constant need for the whole community of faith to repent, to turn back to God, to be washed, cleansed, and made pure once again. This is the path of sanctification. It's like climbing a mountain. You get dirty along the way and you might fall and get bruised. Then you come upon a fresh stream to wash, bind up your wounds, and continue onward and upward.

Leviticus reminds us that the act of salvation is not complete in the Old Testament without the response of God's people to live together in obedience, love, and holiness in every aspect of life. The same is true for Christians in response to the grace of Christ. A believer cannot receive liberation from sin and death without actively participating in the life of the church to serve others in love and purity.

Now that we have a little bit of background on Leviticus and the call to a holy life, we can prepare ourselves to enter into this ancient text. We will get to know the inhabitants and begin to see life from their perspective. We will encounter a people who see the world filled with God's presence and live their daily lives as if standing on holy ground. This is not a people who worship creation, but they witness the presence of the divine in all of creation. They see their role in the drama of salvation and, like actors in a play, they take their part alongside the rest of God's creatures.

To understand Leviticus we too must discover and experience the sacred beauty of God and his creation, our own role in the drama of salvation, and the new creation that is springing up around us. Though at times Leviticus may be puzzling, beneath the surface lies the beauty of the gospel of God's love for his people and his love for the world.

2

Too Much Blood

Understanding Sacrifice and Atonement

THE POWER OF RITUAL

To understand any culture, it's imperative to recognize the signs and symbols that convey meaning to its people. Whether it's the words they use, the rituals they perform, or how they treat one another, all of these provide insights into how they live in community and how they relate to God. So the first stop on our journey will be to explore ritual, sacrifice, and the meaning of blood. Sounds gruesome, but we'll find that it's within these signs and symbols that we can begin to understand how God was teaching his people about the depths of his holiness and forgiveness and why this is so critical in helping make sense of Christ's atoning sacrifice on the cross.

Unlike other books of the Bible, Leviticus is shaped primarily by ritual. Much of the teaching is embedded within the practice of worship and the physical things you do when you come before a holy God. This can be challenging for many Christians. If you come from a Protestant background, you may have been raised with a negative attitude toward rituals. This may stem from the early Reformers, who rallied against some of the practices and rituals of the medieval Roman Catholic church.

For other Christians, interpreting rituals is difficult because they are much more familiar with the New Testament Gospels or Epistles. The stories of Jesus' life or direct instructions from the apostles are much easier to grasp. We can read them in bits and pieces and walk away with a clear understanding of what we're supposed to do to live a faithful life. This, however, is not the case when interpreting ritual.

To understand ritual is to understand an *embodied theology*. This means that every movement, every act, every word pronounced is filled with symbolic meaning. What we do with our bodies becomes an outward expression of what we believe in our hearts. If someone gets down on their knees to pray, their physical posture conveys an inner humility before God. This simple ritual is an outward sign that demonstrates our inward attitude toward the one who is Lord over all creation. Yet the physical act of kneeling also helps shape our belief and reinforces our sense of submission to God. We perform the ritual because of what we believe, but the ritual also helps strengthen and reinforce that belief.

Leviticus teaches us that the path to holiness requires us to believe with our hearts and to express that belief with our bodies. Ritual practice is key to the pursuit of holiness because it reminds us that we are physical creatures who learn through embodied acts of worship. We discover who God is, and who we are as human beings, through these daily acts that become embedded in our lives. Though many might think of ritual as dry, empty repetition, sometimes it is only through the repeated act that we actually begin to learn. It's like playing a musical instrument. The dull, often tedious repetition of practicing scales seems pointless until we realize that the practice has paid off when learning to master a new piece of music. In a similar manner, Leviticus presents physical rituals as a means to "practicing" our faith that lead us to discover God's holiness and help us on the path to purity.

We might think of rituals as something confined to the religious world, but rituals help form our everyday lives whether we realize it or not. Dru Johnson, in his book *Human Rites*, explores how we practice daily rituals often without recognizing why we do things or what we express by doing them. If we believe that we're exposed to dangerous germs in the world we might frequently wash our hands throughout the day or wear a mask in public places. We might develop patterns of taking vitamins every morning because we believe they're good for our health even if, in some instances, they might have little or no effect. Many have coffee rituals in the morning (myself included!) that convey the underlying belief that a hot drink with caffeine is the only way to start the day.

Oftentimes rituals are created when "normal" events are transformed to take on special significance. A normal family meal is transformed into an extravagant feast at a wedding banquet. A shower or bath can be turned into a rite of purification or the ritual of baptism in the Christian church. A funeral is a ritualized act of people gathering together to mourn someone's death. The Eucharist takes a simple meal of bread and wine and changes it into a ritual that teaches about Christ's death and resurrection.[1] Whether religious or not, we perform rituals each day that not only *express* what we believe, but also *shape* how we believe by how we act.

Johnson goes on to say, "But maybe we don't need to understand how rituals work *on* us in order for them to work *in* us."[2] This is the real power of ritual. What we do teaches us to see and experience the world through embodied action. Oftentimes we might not understand *how* a ritual affects us, but we are nonetheless changed the more we practice the ritual action.

Think about the rituals we go through in learning to ride a bike. When we first get on, we have to think about everything we do. We try to balance this strange, two-wheeled machine while pedaling with our feet and steering with our hands. Shaking, swerving, tottering, we're engaging mind and body to stay upright and propel ourselves forward without crashing (not always successfully!). In the beginning we have to think constantly about how to keep ourselves safe, how to signal when we turn, or how to avoid a pothole. However, once we've practiced the ritual over and over, we no longer think about each pedal stroke or keeping our balance. Our minds can drift off to think about other things as we navigate our way through the countryside and enjoy the sun or a strong tailwind. The embodied action has taught us how to stay safe and allows us to experience a ride in a completely new way.

Though there are many positive aspects to ritual, not all rituals are healthy. A person who smokes two packs of cigarettes every day creates a deadly pattern that may lead to lung cancer. A person who is addicted to shopping buys new things not out of necessity, but because they have been lured into the consumerism of our age. How we dress each day or how much makeup we put on might be an unhealthy expression of low self-esteem or how we're trying to impress others. Some may develop dangerous eating habits because of similar feelings of inadequacy that may be the result of constant exposure to social media or advertisements telling us we need to look a certain way to be happy. Whatever rituals we have in our lives, they establish patterns that *express* what we believe inwardly and *enforce* those beliefs through embodied action.

Though we may not think we're controlled by our rituals, they form a blueprint for reality that helps us make sense of the world. They offer

1. Johnson, *Human Rites*, 21–25.
2. Johnson, *Human Rites*, 53.

symbols that help us grow as human beings and provide rites of passage that help us mature and mark important occasions. Graduations, award ceremonies, baptisms, bar mitzvahs, singing the national anthem before a sporting event; all of these embodied acts both express and form something of our worldview.

I remember as a child in elementary school having to stand facing the flag with hand over heart as we all recited, "I pledge allegiance to the flag . . . ." To this day I find it difficult not to place my hand over my heart when the national anthem is sung and the American flag is flown. As a citizen of the United States, this simple ritual act shapes part of my worldview. The rest of the pledge follows, ". . . and to the republic for which is stands, one nation under God, indivisible, with liberty and justice for all." Though most Americans fall short of these aspirations, they express a fundamental view that all human beings under God deserve liberty and justice and that I must somehow play my part in that goal as a faithful citizen.

So how does this all connect to Leviticus? To understand this book of the Bible, in order to see into the world of ancient Israel, we need to grasp what rituals do and why we perform them. We need to examine the symbols, the rites, and every bodily movement as it is described to help in our understanding of what beliefs they might represent. We need to figure out how the drama of things like sacrifice unfold before the offeror and the priest and what this teaches about God and our relationship to him as human beings. This, I believe, is partly why so many people avoid Leviticus and think it too strange and foreign a book. In reality it's no more foreign than encountering a different culture that requires us to learn a new language, understand different symbols, values, and rituals to truly grasp how others perceive the world.

As we explore ritual in further depth, we'll start with one of the most powerful symbols known to humanity—*blood*. Some of you may already want to stop reading, but if you really want to get to the heart of God's teaching in Leviticus and his desire for atonement and reconciliation then it all starts with blood. The rituals of blood sacrifice that God gave his people would shape their worship and belief for over a thousand years before the Jerusalem temple was finally destroyed in 70 AD by the Romans. Only then did sacrifices cease, but their legacy continues to have an impact on Judaism and Christianity today.

THE LIFE IS IN THE BLOOD

Killing an animal as an offering to God for the sake of atonement is about as foreign a concept to our modern Western culture as we could possibly imagine. What would God want with a poor, innocent animal and why would he command such inhumane slaughtering of his own creation? What may seem to us a sign of religious superstition was, in fact, a central practice among nearly all cultures in the ancient world.

Blood was seen as the substance of life and for Israel's neighbors it was often used for magic or for sacrifices to manipulate or appease the gods. In an effort to alleviate some of the hardships experienced in the ancient world, blood was seen as the most precious gift for the gods that had the potential to influence their behavior and possibly bring blessing. Sadly, at times, this led some cultures to offer the most precious blood, that of a child, as a sacrifice to their gods. There are indications that even Israel fell into such terrible practices (see Lev 18:21; 20:2–5; Jer 32:35). Yet this use of blood is resolutely condemned by God throughout the Old Testament.

The reason that God despised such sacrifices is because *all blood* and *all life* belong to him. This idea goes back to the days of Noah, when God commands him not to eat meat with the blood (Gen 9:4–6) and that to do so is tantamount to murder. So strong was this tradition regarding blood, we see the apostles who gathered together in Jerusalem give simple instructions for how gentiles could live by faith in Jesus. After hearing stories of gentile conversions from Paul and Barnabas, the apostle James says that these new believers should, "abstain only from things polluted by idols and from fornication and from whatever has been strangled and from blood" (Acts 15:20). The decision to refrain "from blood" stems directly from the traditions in Genesis and the instructions found in Leviticus.

One of the key verses in Leviticus that helps us understand the strange world of blood and sacrifice in the Bible is Lev 17:11:

> For the life of the flesh is in the blood; and I have given it to you
> for making atonement for your lives on the altar; for, as life, it is
> the blood that makes atonement.

Most of the rituals in Leviticus don't offer any explanation, but this is one of the rare instances where something is spelled out for us, which means we need to pay close attention.

All living things are created by the hands of God and within the flesh of each creature is this mysterious red substance that symbolizes its life. The creature's life can only and ever belong to God since he is the source of all life. Blood is always to be treated as precious and never to be abused by human beings. It must be handled with extreme care in any situation, but especially when it is presented as an offering. In fact, Leviticus expressly states that *all sacrificial* blood should only be shed on God's altar (Lev 17:1–9). We can infer from the later comments about the Israelites making sacrifices in the "open field" (17:5) or to the "goat demons" (17:7) that the people were following the practices of the Canaanites. Yet Leviticus teaches that God is the only giver of life and the substance of life (i.e., blood) should always return to him.[3]

Whereas other cultures used blood for different rites or ceremonies, Israel is given blood strictly for the sake of atonement on the altar. Blood is the only substance that carries the potency of life and it is the only thing that has the power to purge death. It's as if God is saying to his people, "I'm giving you blood as a gift so that even when you die in your sin, you can be forgiven and made alive in your relationship with me. Blood is not for my benefit, but for yours."

This teaches Israel that with sin comes death and that freedom from death is through life. The author of the letter to the Hebrews reminds his readers that, "under the law almost everything is purified with blood, and without the shedding of blood there is no forgiveness of sins" (Heb 9:22). Therefore, the life of the animal, represented by its blood, is the antidote that can cleanse us from death, purify us, and allow us to return to God's holy presence. Death brings uncleanness and separation—blood has the power to purify and bring us back into union with God.

One way to think about sin is that it's like a stain that covers part of us. No matter how hard we try to get rid of the stain, we can't do it on our own. And that stain is something that prevents us from being able to approach God's purity and holiness. But if the blood of atonement is shed on our behalf, the life within that blood cleanses the stain, purifies us, and allows us to come back into relationship with God. This is one of the reasons why Leviticus is so concerned with the symbols and rituals of animal sacrifice—they express the deepest and most powerful means we have in restoring our relationship to a holy God.

But couldn't God have used something else besides blood to forgive sins? Why did Israel have to go through the whole process of killing animals? I suppose God could have used other means to teach his people about sin, death, atonement, and reconciliation, but blood was a universal symbol of power and life in the ancient world. God was taking the signs that were already deeply embedded within the human psyche to reveal their true meaning to his people. Leviticus takes a symbol that had been frequently

---

3. Leviticus is mainly concerned with blood in the context of sacrifice at God's altar. Murder, like in the story of Cain and Abel (Gen 4:1–16), is an unjust shedding of blood. Human beings are made in God's image and will be held accountable for taking the life (blood) of another human being. In some circumstances, however, bloodshed in battle is considered justified, especially if it is sanctioned by God.

perverted by human beings and baptizes it, as it were, by redefining blood as a gift from God only to be used for atonement at his altar.

Lastly, blood can also be seen as a source of contamination. Though blood is associated with life, it can also be a sign of death that makes a person ritually unclean. There are various commands around women menstruating (Lev 15:19–30) or discharging blood after childbirth (Lev 12:4–8) which we'll discuss in chapter 5 on the purity laws. The loss of blood in these examples is identified with the fragile balance between life and death. The commands regarding uncleanness due to the natural functions of a woman's body were not a moral or ethical judgement against her. Instead, they represent a belief that the blood of our bodies, even through natural discharge, somehow makes us ritually unclean for a certain time before we can approach God's holiness once again.

THE DRAMA OF SACRIFICE

The power of ritual to teach through embodied action is key to understanding why there is so much detail devoted to sacrifice in the first section of Leviticus. Chapters 1–7 offer a seemingly exhaustive list of different offerings, with endless repetition about how an animal is to be butchered, which parts belong to God, where blood is sprinkled, and what is to be burned on the altar. It's no wonder that most people struggle when reading through Leviticus! These are possibly the least inviting chapters of any book of the Bible, but when we look at them through the lens of ritual and try to understand their symbolism, we begin to see how God was teaching his people about forgiveness and atonement through the drama of sacrifice.

Just imagine for a moment that you've never had any formal education, you grew up working on a small farm with your family, you don't know how to read or write, and anything you've been taught about God has been from your parents. Then one day your father takes you by the hand and tells you that the family needs to make a sacrifice because they have committed a sin unintentionally by not following God's commands.

On your way up to the temple your father explains to you that sin results in death and that the blood of an animal is the only way for the family to be forgiven and reconciled with God. He reminds you that the life in the blood is a gift from God so that his people can remain in relationship with him.

As you're walking along, you look down at the spotless lamb that you've taken care of since it was born. A simple creature that has lived in your household its whole life who must now become a sacrifice so that you, and God's temple, might be cleansed. You can't imagine how this is going to take place, but you sense a seriousness in your father's voice that you've never heard before and realize something significant is happening.

When you arrive at the temple other people from different villages and clans are making their offerings. Your senses are overwhelmed by the sounds of all the animals, the sight of smoke and fire rising up from the outer altar, and the smell of burnt flesh. You watch the priests methodically moving around as they sprinkle blood on the horns extending from the top of the altar and at its base. They look like holy butchers as their clothes are saturated and stained red with blood spilling and spurting everywhere.

Finally it's your turn. You approach with your father, bowing in reverence as you draw nearer toward the altar. The priest holds the lamb and you watch as your father lays a hand on its head for a moment that seems like an eternity. Then your father holds the lamb as the priest skillfully and exactly slits the throat of the animal. You watch as the blood gushes out on the ground and into the brass pot below while the animal's body goes limp. The lamb that you brought alive and breathing is now gone. The lamb you watched birthed into this world has given its life for your sake, for the sake of your family, and for the sake of the whole community.

The priest then goes about finishing the removal of the fat and different body parts and places them on the altar. You witness a living creature turned into smoke and ash as its physical remains ascend to the heavens as a pleasing offering to the Lord. The sight, the sounds, the smells will remain etched in your memory forever and will remind you of the holiness of God, of his provision for the forgiveness of sin, and the preciousness of life and blood as it's used for the cleansing and atonement of God's people.

Though the story above is fictional, it's based on the prescriptions of Leviticus 4 and the purification offerings for unintentional sins. Every act is filled with symbolism and carries meaning. One thing we note at the start is that the offeror plays a key role in the drama. Though the priest will perform the sacrifice, the offeror is the one who places a hand on the animal before it's slaughtered. The meaning of this is debated, but it's likely that the act represents the identification of the person with the offering. Placing one hand on the animal is like saying before God, "I identify my life and my sin with the life and blood of this animal that I offer to you." The offeror and the sacrifice are bound together so that when God receives the burnt offering, he also receives and forgives the offeror.

Then the lamb's throat is slit in the cleanest, most efficient way possible. The point of sacrifice is not to inflict pain on the animal, but to offer its life on behalf of another. In fact, later rabbinic instructions for slaughter require that everything be done to make sure the animal is calm and that its death is as quick and painless as possible. The priest then takes the bowl of blood and dips his finger in and puts it on the horns that extend from the corners of the altar. This is another sign of purification, wiping away the sin of God's people from his holy place.

The purification of the sanctuary is as significant as the purification of the sinner in Leviticus. The priests atone for *the altar* and for the *whole community* of Israel (Lev 8:15; 16:33). After this the fatty portions of the animal are separated and burned. The symbols of smoke and fire convey the physical and spiritual transference of the offering to God.

The drama of sacrifice was a way for Israel to worship and to learn about the holiness of their God. The prescribed rituals made them participate physically in the ongoing drama of salvation, reconciliation, and forgiveness. In a time when very few people were literate and there was limited access to the written word, God teaches his people through ritual and an embodied faith.

Eugene Peterson recalls growing up in a church where the pastor preached for three months on Leviticus. Having grown up on a farm and having spent time at a local slaughterhouse, he thought this was a book of the Bible that he could surely connect with. But after a few Sundays he lost interest because the pastor had never experienced killing an animal and had missed the "rich sensuality of Hebrew worship." He goes on to write:

> Our pastor had it all figured out on paper, but I knew it wasn't like that at all. I couldn't help but wonder how much he knew about sin and forgiveness. He certainly knew nothing about animal sacrifice. Sacrifice was messy: blood sloshing on the floor, gutting the creatures and gathering up the entrails in buckets, skinning the animals, salting down the hides. And in the summertime, the flies—flies everywhere.[4]

Peterson's reflection is an important one for the study of Leviticus. If we haven't witnessed or participated in the killing of an animal, we're missing the most critical layer of the drama that God creates to teach his people. The sights, the smells, the guttural reaction to blood pouring out, and the sound of an animal before its last breath are all part of understanding what takes place in atonement.

It's important to recall that there were no schools or universities in ancient Israel. But there were rituals and priests who were taught how to perform them to help Israel understand that sin in the presence of a holy God is no small thing. Atonement requires sacrifice. It requires blood and the drama of death for the sake of purity and holiness.

4. Peterson, *The Pastor*, 37–38.

Not all the sacrifices in Leviticus 1–7 were for the purification of sin. There were other offerings as well and possibly the most common in the Old Testament was the "burnt offering" (Lev 1:3–17). This was where the entire animal was burnt on the altar and represented the most complete sacrifice to God since no part of the animal was left for consumption by the priest or the offeror. Most often this was given to God as a sign of joy or thanksgiving or possibly to avert God's punishment, as David does to stop the plague devastating Jerusalem (2 Sam 24:21–25).

Other sacrifices like the "grain offering" was something that was shared with the priests. This is described in detail in Leviticus 2 and represents a less costly form of worship for those who could not afford an animal. This type of offering was seen as a tribute or gift to God out of thanksgiving for his faithfulness and provision.

Another type of offering is often called the "peace offering" because of the Hebrew word *shalom*, but it could also be translated as "well-being offering" or "wholeness offering" (Lev 3:1–17). This was an offering of thanksgiving for the wholeness or peace that Israel experienced with God and with their neighbor. This sacrifice was different, in that part of the animal was given to God, but the other parts were divided between the priest and the offeror. Specific details are given for the division of the animal, but things like the fat, a symbol of the richest portion, were always given to God alone (Lev 3:16–17).

In other offerings, such as the "guilt offering" or "reparation offering," the person had to make a sacrifice *and* make amends with their neighbor. In this instance the sacrifice alone did not free the offender of their guilt since they were often required to make restitution of an extra 20 percent (Lev 6:1–7). Here we see the connection between the ethical and ritual. The act of sacrifice alone does not restore us to relationship with God if we neglect reconciliation with our neighbor. Jesus highlights this in the Sermon on the Mount when he says, "So when you are offering your gift at the altar, if you remember that your brother or sister has something against you, leave your gift there before the altar and go; first be reconciled to your brother or sister, and then come and offer your gift" (Matt 5:23–24). The ritual offering must always be accompanied by ethical living.

Throughout the different seasons Israel also gave their daily offerings, their tithes, and first fruits or offerings around harvest. Each of these were given as a gift to God, acknowledging his grace and blessing in the provision he provided for his people. All of these instructions show how God tethered the life of his people to his altar through ritual and sacrifice. Every act, every movement, every prayer uttered (though, strangely, Leviticus makes no mention of specific prayers with sacrifices), teaches Israel that they are bound to a holy God who loves them and makes his presence and blessing known by dwelling in their midst.

It's not uncommon for people to read through the first chapters of Leviticus and feel like it's just a cold, technical manual on how ancient Israelites offered sacrifices. But if we read it through the lens of ritual, drama, and symbolism we begin to see how every detail expresses some sort of theological meaning. We also see how these rituals draw the community of faith together around the altar to remind them that the God who abides with them is holy. In a non-literate culture these physical acts performed within the divine drama served as powerful reminders of Israel's ongoing need for purification and reconciliation. They also remind Israel what it means to live together as a covenant people, praising their God for his blessings and approaching his altar with their gifts.

We may not have had the experience of slaughtering an animal, but to understand the depths of Leviticus we need to read, at the very least, with our imaginations opened. We need to think about the physical senses that were engaged in sacrifice and try our best to imagine what it might have felt like to worship in the ways God commanded. If we read Leviticus like a textbook, we'll struggle to grasp how God was teaching his people through the power of ritual. But if we seek to discern the signs and symbols, a new world of holiness will open before our eyes.

THE DAY OF ATONEMENT

The climax of all sacrifice in Leviticus is the Day of Atonement or *Yom Kippur*. The details of the festival are laid out in Leviticus 16. The entire chapter is devoted to the precise movements and actions that Aaron, the high priest, must perform to cleanse both the tabernacle and the Israelites of their sin. Though sacrifices for sin occur throughout the year, the Day of Atonement is a complete purging of all the residue and stain that has been left on the tabernacle from the sins of the people.

When thinking about the effects of sin in Leviticus, it's important to remember that we're not just talking about something that causes personal, spiritual death. Of course, sin does create death in our hearts, but that was not the primary way that the ancient Israelites understood sin. They conceived of sin as a force that leads the world back into a state of chaos. In the first chapter we spoke about the goodness and beauty of God's creation that was "saved" by his bringing order to the world out of chaos. When sin enters the world, it's as if that order breaks down and leads humanity and creation back toward destruction.

Sin was not something that merely had personal consequences. It affected the individual, the community, the land, and especially the tabernacle. This is a difficult concept for us to understand today because sin has largely become privatized in our modern world. We think that if we sin and no one knows about it, then the consequences are between us and God. If I ask for personal forgiveness in my personal prayers, that should be enough and then I can get on with life. In Leviticus, however, sin is a force that has a very real impact on those around us and on the physical world. Whether sin is intentional or unintentional, it's not something that can be hidden away because it will ultimately have adverse effects on the whole community of faith.

God's instructions for the Day of Atonement give us a clue as to why these sacrifices must happen once a year in the innermost space of the tabernacle—the holy of holies. God commands the high priest, "Thus he shall make atonement for the sanctuary, because of the uncleannesses of the people of Israel, and because of their transgressions, all their sins; and so he shall do for the tent of meeting, which remains with them in the midst of their uncleannesses" (Lev 16:16). Atonement for sin was done primarily for the sake of cleansing the physical space of the tabernacle where God dwelt. This means that there was something like a physical residue of Israel's sin that needed to be cleansed every year. This might be even harder for us to wrap our minds around. How can an inward sin committed in my heart or mind, like coveting, have a physical effect on God's dwelling place?

This is where we need to think about Israel's understanding of the *materiality of sin*. The idea is that sin is pictured as a physical substance which is somehow connected to the physical and spiritual world. Sin has the potential to contaminate physical space. Consequently, if one sins we might picture a stain or blemish that somehow rests on God's holy dwelling place. A person's uncleanness causes God's home to become unclean. And the more that the pictured substance of sin contaminates God's house, the greater the possibility that he will leave because he cannot dwell in the uncleanness of sin. Though there were no literal physical stains from sin on the tabernacle, the Israelites perceived its contaminating effects and so made sacrifices to cleanse God's holy space.

Christians are used to understanding sin as a spiritual concept that affects the individual heart or soul. But imagine if your sin, even your most private thoughts, had a negative effect on your church and your church community. Imagine if every sin by those in the congregation stained the church and somehow left it unclean. Then imagine that the sins of the community built up so much throughout the year that you feared that the Holy Spirit might be driven away. This is how ancient Israel understood their sin in relation to the tabernacle and why there was a need for this purging every year.

Let's take a look at what actually happened on the Day of Atonement. This is the only day of the year on which the high priest, and only the high priest, can enter the holy of holies. His instructions are to go in before the ark of the covenant and the mercy seat, which sits on top of the ark, to offer sacrifices to atone for himself, his family, and for the sins of the Israelites (Lev 16:2–19). He is also to bring two goats to the entrance and cast lots (like rolling dice) over them to decide which one is to be sacrificed to the Lord and which one is to be sent into the wilderness to Azazel.

When the high priest presents the offering in the holy of holies he does so with a censer full of burning incense to create a cloud over the mercy seat, "so that he does not die" (Lev 16:13). Approaching the holiness of God is not something to be taken lightly. He then takes some of the blood and sprinkles it on the east side of the mercy seat and in front seven times. Then he does the same with the blood of the goat. Afterwards he performs a similar rite on the altar in the outer court.

When the sacrifices are complete and the tabernacle has been cleansed and purged of the substance of sin, the high priest takes the goat for Azazel. Here is where we find one of those rare explanations of a ritual.

> Then Aaron shall lay both his hands on the head of the live goat, and confess over it all the iniquities of the people of Israel, and all their transgressions, all their sins, putting them on the head of the goat, and sending it away into the wilderness by means of someone designated for the task. The goat shall bear on itself all their iniquities to a barren region; and the goat shall be set free in the wilderness. (Lev 16:21–22)

We remember that an offering for atonement required the offeror to place one hand on the animal as a sign of identification with its life, but here we're told specifically that Aaron places two hands on the goat as an act of transference, placing all of Israel's sins on the goat. Though the act of atonement and cleansing has already taken place in the tabernacle, the scapegoat becomes the physical vehicle through which Israel's sins are symbolically removed from their presence.

The scapegoat ritual has been recorded in other ancient civilizations. The idea of an animal bearing sin or disease to save others is a powerful archetype and visual for the removal of guilt. It was an act that all the Israelites would have witnessed as they watched the high priest place his hands on the goat and then drive it into the wilderness and possibly push it over a cliff. With their sin atoned for by the sacrifices of the high priest, and their guilt disposed of through the scapegoat, the Israelites could rejoice that God had forgiven them and would remain with them in his sanctuary.

The question you might be asking at this point is, who is Azazel? There are various theories, but the likelihood is that it represents some sort of demon who symbolizes the chaos of the desert. We're given a clue later in Lev 17:7, which prohibits Israel's practice of sacrificing to "goat demons," but other than that the text assumes a common knowledge of who Azazel is. In later Jewish writings during the Second Temple period (ca. 400–100 BCE), the apocryphal book of 1 *Enoch* identifies Azazel as one of the fallen angels who corrupts humanity. Most likely Azazel represents the forces of sin and chaos and the symbol of the goat becomes a visual reminder of Israel's sin being cast back to its place of origin.

When we step back and think about the power of ritual, the symbolic gestures, and participating in the divine drama, we can begin to see how God was teaching his people about the nature of sin, death, sacrifice, atonement, and holiness. The ritual of the Day of Atonement brings together identification, purification, and substitution in one act that marks the moment in time when God fully restores his relationship with his people. Atonement allows for his holiness to be present, to abide in the heart of his community, and to bring the blessings of his promise.

One thing that's noteworthy in the Day of Atonement, and in other sacrifices for sin, is that there is no mention of God's anger. Never do we get the sense that blood or offerings somehow appease the wrath of God. In fact, God's "anger" is only mentioned in Lev 10:6 when he tells Aaron not to mourn the death of his son and in Lev 26:28 where his hostility is aroused by Israel's disobedience. In Leviticus the most fundamental reason for atonement is not to appease God's wrath, but to purify his people and his sanctuary so that they might remain in relationship with him.

There are, of course, other stories in the Bible where sin incites God's anger and judgment. We recall the story of the Golden Calf where Israel was stuck by God's plague (Exod 32:1–10, 35), or the rebellion of the sons of Korah against Moses' leadership (Numbers 16), who were also killed by a plague. We remember Moses creating the bronze serpent to spare Israel from God's punishment (Num 21:4–9), or the plague sent upon them for their sacrificing to foreign gods at Baal of Peor (Num 25:1–9). All of these responses to sin demonstrate God's anger and judgment but none of them call for atoning sacrifices. There are very few stories in the Old Testament where blood sacrifices are made to avoid God's wrath (cf. 1 Sam 14:31–35; 2 Sam 24:10–25).

To understand atonement in Leviticus we must look to the rituals, the symbols, and the instructions God gives concerning his holy tabernacle. We can briefly sum up some of the most important points. 1) God is holy and we are separated from that holiness when we fail to walk according to his commands. 2) Sin, whether intentional or unintentional, leads to chaos and death. Sin creates a stain on the sinner and on God's sanctuary, which must be cleansed if communion with God is to continue. 3) Blood is the only substance powerful enough to purify and purge sin. Because the life is in the blood, and blood is given for atonement, sacrifice is the only way for an unholy people to be cleansed so that they might remain in relationship with God.

ATONEMENT IN THE NEW TESTAMENT

Having explored some of the fundamental building blocks for atonement in Leviticus, how then do we apply these to our understanding of the atoning sacrifice of Christ? Over the centuries there have been different approaches to atonement that have emphasized certain aspects of what happened on the cross. Some focus on the victory of Christ and the cosmic purification achieved by his blood. Others concentrate on the economic side of redemption and our debt being paid through Christ. But for many Christian traditions today the notion of "substitutionary atonement" with Christ taking on our penalty is commonly held. This approach tends to focus on the courtroom metaphor with God sitting as a judge who demands just penalty for individual human sinfulness, but Christ steps in to take on our punishment.[5]

The idea in this approach is that sin is an offense to God that must be punished or paid for to satisfy his justice. God can't arbitrarily forgive sin since that would go against his nature, so his wrath is constantly directed against his people for their inability to pay their debt or suffer their punishment. In this picture, God appears like a ruthless judge in the heavens who cares for little else besides justice. In order to fulfill that justice, God requires a substitution who will suffer under his violent punishment as a payment for sin.

You may have grown up with this type of theology in your own tradition. Christ's atoning sacrifice is seen as appeasing God's wrath as he takes on the punishment of the divine judge for the world. The language of substitution, payment of debt, and forgiveness of sin are all part of the New Testament's language used to describe what happened on the cross, but does this give us the full picture of atonement, especially in relation to what we have seen in Leviticus?

Part of the difficulty with the idea that Christ's atonement was to appease God's wrath is that nowhere in God's prescriptions for atonement in Leviticus is there ever the sense that sacrifices are to satisfy his anger or judgement. God is not depicted as the divine Judge but, rather, he is seen

---

5. See McNall, *The Mosaic of Atonement*.

as the holy and merciful Father who longs to dwell in relationship with his people. In order for his holiness to remain with them, he gives the gift of blood for atonement and cleansing. This teaches Israel about the consequences of sin and its effects on the community and the tabernacle. The sacrificial system was not primarily a vehicle to avoid God's wrath and judgement but, rather, it was established so that Israel could be purified from sin and remain in communion with him.

This is not to say that Leviticus was unconcerned with God's justice or judgement. The opposite is true. Leviticus is very clear that God is holy *and* just and that he will judge the people according to their sins (cf. Lev 26:14–39). What it doesn't express is that blood, atonement, and sacrifice are about satisfying God's justice or appeasing his wrath. Instead, the focus of the sacrificial system is primarily on holiness, purity, atonement, and forgiveness that leads to the possibility of relationship.

Another problem with the idea that sacrifice is a penalty paid for sin relates to how we understand the animal's role in sacrifice. Leviticus does not present the view that an animal is somehow taking on the penalty or punishment deserved by the offeror. Instead, the person identifies with the life in the blood that is given to cleanse sin. If the life in the blood was *primarily for cleansing the tabernacle*, then the concept of atonement moves beyond personal forgiveness to purification for the benefit of the entire community. Atoning sacrifices were not only given so that the individual could avoid punishment but, rather, they were for the sake of the whole community's purity so that God might remain in their midst.

When we take some of these principles of sacrifice and atonement in Leviticus and apply them to our understanding of Christ's sacrifice, we begin to recognize the wider implications of the cross. If we focus solely on Christ's death as a satisfaction for the penalty of *my* sins, we restrict the cross to a personal remedy. If, however, we see the cross through the rituals and symbols of God's instruction in Leviticus then we see Christ's sacrifice primarily as a cleansing and purification of the heavenly tabernacle that includes the whole of creation.

This is the vision that Paul conveys in his letter to the believers in Colossae.

> He himself is before all things, and in him all things hold together. He is the head of the body, the church; he is the beginning, the firstborn from the dead, so that he might come to have first place in everything. For in him all the fullness of God was pleased to dwell, and through him God was pleased to reconcile

to himself all things, whether on earth or in heaven, by making peace through the blood of his cross. (Col 1:17–20)

All things are reconciled in peace because of the super-abundance of life found in the blood that is both human and divine. It is only Christ's blood that can make atonement for God's cosmic tabernacle, the whole of the heavens and the earth.

We find a similar message in the epistle to the Hebrews where the author offers an extended discussion of the earthly tabernacle and its symbolism preparing the way for Christ, the great high priest. "But when Christ came as a high priest of the good things that have come, then through the greater and perfect tent (not made with hands, that is, not of this creation), he entered once for all into the Holy Place, not with the blood of goats and calves, but with his own blood, thus obtaining eternal redemption" (Heb 9:11–12). The author goes on, and it's worth quoting this in full as it sums up Christ's sacrifice in light of what we have discussed above.

> Thus it was necessary for the sketches of the heavenly things to be purified with these rites, but the heavenly things themselves need better sacrifices than these. For Christ did not enter a sanctuary made by human hands, a mere copy of the true one, but he entered into heaven itself, now to appear in the presence of God on our behalf. Nor was it to offer himself again and again, as the high priest enters the Holy Place year after year with blood that is not his own; for then he would have had to suffer again and again since the foundation of the world. But as it is, he has appeared once for all at the end of the age to remove sin by the sacrifice of himself. And just as it is appointed for mortals to die once, and after that the judgment, so Christ, having been offered once to bear the sins of many, will appear a second time, not to deal with sin, but to save those who are eagerly waiting for him. (Heb 9:23–28)

This is the hope of Christ's sacrifice—that he has purified the cosmic tabernacle of the heavens and the earth by his atoning blood. He has eliminated the stain of sin and death by his sacrifice and has allowed all people to draw near to his holiness through the gift of the Holy Spirit in confidence and full assurance of faith.

If Christ's sacrifice was once-for-all then what happens to the commands of Leviticus concerning sacrifice and the temple? The epistle to the Hebrews goes to great lengths to demonstrate how Jesus has fulfilled the sacrificial system and why it is no longer needed in the age of the church.

But there were other factors that brought an end to blood sacrifice in Jerusalem, namely the destruction of the temple by the Romans in 70 AD.

From that time onward there was a gradual movement among Jews toward prayer as a substitute for the offering of daily sacrifices. Rather than shedding blood, Jews around the Mediterranean and throughout the Middle East gathered in synagogues to study Torah and pray as their offering of worship. The Jerusalem temple was, and still is, a central part of faith for many Jews, but the ancient practice of sacrifices at the altar was transformed into a life of fervent prayer and the study of Torah.

For Christians, the once-for-all sacrifice of Christ resulted in the purification and cleansing of all sin. This brought an end to ritual offerings in the temple and fulfilled the Levitical sacrificial system. Yet Christ also created a new ritual for a new covenant that reveals a deeper meaning of offering blood and flesh for atonement.

In the upper room on the eve of the Passover, Jesus reimagines the seder meal that looked forward to God's liberation and future salvation. Using the sacrificial images of flesh and blood through the physical elements of bread and wine, Jesus institutes (in good Levitical fashion!) a ritual to be performed by his disciples and all who follow him to remember his suffering, death, resurrection, and ascension.

The transformation of the Passover meal into the Eucharist offers a profound vision and ritual that links back to Exodus and Leviticus yet anticipates the cross and ultimately a final reconciliation that is being established through the work and unity of Christ's body, the church. We remember that in Leviticus the blood of the animal was only sprinkled on the altar for atonement and never on the individual, but Jesus hands his disciples the cup of wine and says, "Drink from it, all of you; for this is my blood of the covenant, which is poured out for many for the forgiveness of sins" (Matt 26:27–28). You can imagine the shock of the disciples at the very thought of drinking sacrificial blood! Though it was a symbol for his blood that would be shed on the cross, the thought of consuming blood might have sounded like blasphemy to any faithful Jew.

We can also imagine the shock of the priests in John's Gospel when Jesus alludes to his sacrifice and the institution of the Eucharist.

> Very truly, I tell you, unless you eat the flesh of the Son of Man and drink his blood, you have no life in you. Those who eat my flesh and drink my blood have eternal life, and I will raise them up on the last day; for my flesh is true food and my blood is true drink. Those who eat my flesh and drink my blood abide in me, and I in them. Just as the living Father sent me, and I live

because of the Father, so whoever eats me will live because of me. (John 6:53–57)

Considering how precious and sacred blood is, it is no wonder that the priests and Pharisees thought Jesus was mad.

Christ's institution of the Eucharist deliberately draws on the rituals of Passover in Exodus and blood sacrifice in Leviticus to express an almost incomprehensible truth. If the Israelites experienced reconciliation and relationship with God through the atoning blood of animals, how much more are those reconciled to the Father through the super-atoning blood of Christ. Union with Christ and the Father is now made possible through his sacrifice and the outpouring of the Holy Spirit.

We also remember that in Leviticus the offeror placed a hand on the animal to identify with its life as a gift to God. In a similar manner, the Christian receives the bread and wine to identify with the life and blood of Christ's offering on the cross. Rather than burning the sacrifice up in smoke and fire, the elements of the offering are consumed as they physically and symbolically become one with the Christian worshipper. Simple bread and wine become blood and flesh as signs of Christ's real presence entering into us physically and spiritually so that we might have life in him.

Every time Christians practice the ritual of the Eucharist they are reminded of this truth. Though we may not understand how the ritual works, we remember Dru Johnson's words that "we don't need to understand how rituals work *on* us in order for them to work *in* us." This is part of the mystery of our union with Christ as it is expressed through our participation in the Eucharist. This is the mystery of how the sacrament works in us, through the Spirit, by God's grace. The sign and ritual are necessary for us because it awakens our body, our senses, our heart, and mind to the grace that is working within us. God communicates with us through the ritual drama of the Eucharist to show us that we can embody the inexpressible light and life of Christ.

The ritualized and embodied practice of the Eucharist, instituted by Christ, roots itself in the commands of Leviticus. The Father revealed his holiness and character to Israel through blood, forgiveness, and the cleansing of sin so that they might remain in relationship with him. Just as the Father wanted to teach Israel about holiness and atonement through ritual and sacrifice, so too does Jesus teach the church the same through the Eucharist. At the heart of these rituals is the goal of reconciliation, wholeness, and relationship. Though the blood of animals could not fully achieve this end, the blood of Christ now does.

3

Nuclear Power, Alien Fire, and God's Home on Earth

A NUCLEAR POWER PLANT

With a sense of ritual, sacrifice, and blood we can now move on to see why these things were so critical in relation to God's home on earth—the tabernacle. The decent of the divine to dwell permanently among his people is no small thing, which is why Leviticus is so concerned with defining, and protecting, sacred space. At the epicenter of Israelite life is the tabernacle, the most holy place of God. It's a place that must be maintained appropriately and so God institutes priests in Leviticus to act as its caretakers for the sake of the whole community. We may wonder why God established a priestly institution around the tabernacle, but, as we shall see, the glory that descends to dwell in a tent is a foreshadowing of the glory that will descend and dwell in the flesh of Christ. Jesus will become the tabernacling presence of God on earth and we will witness what happens when God's holiness is made fully manifest in the power of the Son. We will also discover why the priesthood is so critical in the Old Testament as a sign that points to the revelation of Christ as the risen and ascended great high priest.

One of the best illustrations I've heard used to describe the tabernacle is to think of it like a nuclear power plant that is driven by God's holiness. This tent-sanctuary is central to the life of Israel because it's the source of all blessing. It provides the raw energy of God's presence that brings life, wholeness, and peace. But it's also a place of extreme danger because it houses the awesome power of God's holiness that cannot be controlled by humanity. It must, therefore, be approached and handled with extreme care, reverence, and caution.

The generation of nuclear power today is an amazing feat of scientific research. The process of atoms being smashed together is extremely dangerous and yet the outcome of power converted into electricity benefits humanity. The average person never sees the inner workings of a nuclear power plant because it's only for highly trained and skilled professionals to handle things like the uranium needed for atomic reactions.

Nuclear fission is a remarkable, yet highly volatile, operation. When uranium atoms are bombarded by neutrons to be split apart, the division releases neutrons, which in turn collide with other atoms causing a chain reaction. These atomic explosions are harnessed through control rods that absorb the neutrons. The whole process of splitting the uranium atoms releases energy that heats water, which can then be used to spin turbines and produce electricity.

There are significant debates around whether the benefits of nuclear energy outweigh its potential impact on the environment. For the sake of the illustration, however, the power plant represents an energy source that, when contained and treated properly, provides the blessing of electricity to surrounding communities. On the other hand, if not managed correctly, that very same power produced for blessing has the potential to become a devastating curse.

How tragically this was demonstrated in the nuclear meltdown at Chernobyl in April of 1986. The nuclear power plant in the Ukraine experienced an uncontrolled series of chain reactions that led to a core meltdown. This resulted in the release of harmful radioactive contamination that poisoned the land and its inhabitants exceeding a thirty-kilometer radius. Exposure to high levels of radiation led to a rise in rates of thyroid cancer and subsequent generations have suffered from ongoing psychological effects. The land too has been adversely affected with soil and water contamination along with animals of countless species that were killed from the radiation. The effort to decontaminate the area continues today, decades later.

This type of disaster graphically reminds us of the need to have highly skilled, trained professionals working in places that require extreme caution and care to protect the surrounding community. With this image in mind, we can now turn back to Leviticus and the tabernacle space. We shift our thoughts from the core reactor of a nuclear power plant to an ark in the holy of holies and the throne of the Almighty God.

It would not be an exaggeration to say that the ancient Israelites believed the fullness of God's glory resided with them in a small, portable tent. We might think of this as some quaint superstition, but the witness of the Bible and the long portions of Scripture devoted to the design, construction, and consecration of the tabernacle, demonstrate how critical it was as a sign of God's presence with his people. Such a seemingly small and insignificant tent had cosmic implications in the life and faith of God's people because it represented the power of heaven intersecting with earth. The tabernacle space and God's divine presence opened a gateway back to Eden, back to the garden where God and humanity once enjoyed unhindered communion together.

When trying to understand the world of Leviticus it's critical to grasp the idea of sacred space. The heavens and the earth are filled with God's glory, but the *concentrated power* of his holiness is located within the tabernacle. God's home among the Israelites in the form of a portable tent marks an irruption of holiness into the world that fundamentally alters the course of history. God's heavenly throne has been established on earth like a king establishing the rule of his kingdom.

The fiery revelation that began with Moses at the burning bush was magnified on Mt. Sinai in fire, smoke, and lightening when Israel met with their God. This awesome display of glory is then housed in a portable tent for God's people to carry through the wilderness to the promised land where it will eventually rest in the temple of Jerusalem.[1] The tabernacle is the hazardous atomic center of God's holiness that is also the sign and source of salvation for Israel and for all nations.

REIMAGINING EDEN

The design of sacred space is not initiated by the plans or agendas of human beings in the Old Testament. Only God can reveal the detailed blueprints for his divine abode and this is all explained in extraordinary detail to Moses in the book of Exodus. The tabernacle instructions come toward the end of Exodus in chapters 25–31 and then a description of its construction is found in chapters 35–40. It's remarkable to think that almost a third of the book of Exodus is devoted to the tabernacle, but this gives you a sense of its prominence in the story of salvation and its centrality to the life and faith of Israel.

---

1. Eliade, *The Sacred and the Profane*, 26.

One reason why the specific layout is so important is because the tabernacle reflects a microcosm of God's design in creation. As everything in Genesis was neatly divided and ordered by God in the beginning, so too is the tabernacle a precisely ordered space that reflects different grades of holiness.[2] In the diagram below you can see the separation between the inner courtyard and the outer courtyard. Both are symmetrical and are marked by the diagonals to designate the two epicenters of holiness in the altar of the outer courtyard and the ark of the covenant covered with the mercy seat inside the holy of holies. The outer altar was used for daily sacrifices while the inner altar was used only once a year on the Day of Atonement and only by the high priest.

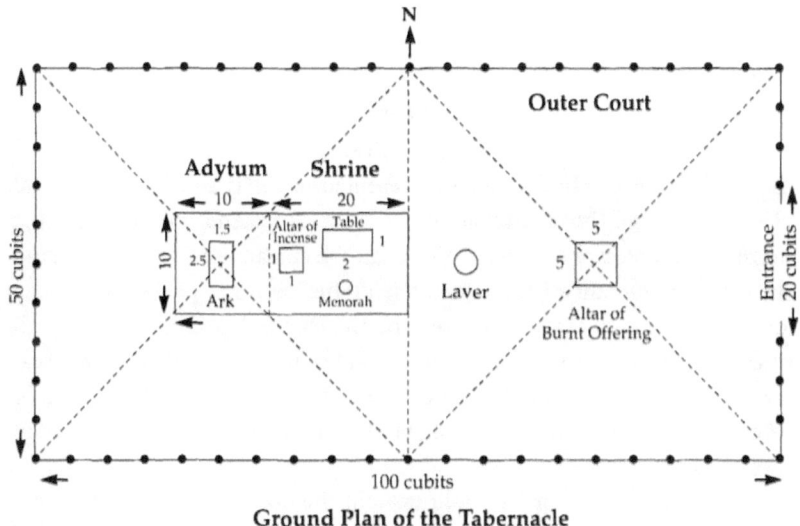

Ground Plan of the Tabernacle

[from Milgrom, *Leviticus 1–16*, 135.]

The furnishings of the tabernacle offer reflections of Eden. The inner courtyard was overlaid in gold and decorated with fabrics of blue, purple, and scarlet died wool that was woven with fine linen and gold. God instructed Moses to embroider cherubim on the curtains (called the *parokhet*) that hung between the holy place (named "Shrine" in the diagram) and the holy of holies (named "Adytum" in the diagram). This was a visible reminder of the garden as we recall the cherubim stationed at the east of Eden with flaming swords to guard its entrance (Gen 3:24). The priests always entered

---

2. See Jenson, *Graded Holiness*.

the tabernacle from the east and passing through the curtain was symbolic of passing through the angelic guards to the place where God dwells.

Inside the holy place there was a menorah, or the seven-branched lampstand with cups that were shaped like almond blossoms. The tree-like image with light shining from the oil in its cups is a reminder of the tree of life in Eden. We don't actually know what the lamp looked like. In fact, many of the items in the tabernacle lack specific detail so we can assume that God inspired the artists through their own craftsmanship and imagination. Though the entire tabernacle reflects God's design, within that space he also allows for human creativity.

The earliest image we have of a menorah is that which was carved on the Arch of Titus in Rome. The grand archway commemorated the Roman sacking and looting of the Jerusalem temple in 70 AD. The menorah remains a powerful symbol in Judaism today and the festival of Hanukkah celebrates its light, which miraculously remained when the Jews recaptured the temple from the Greeks in 167 BCE.

Within the tabernacle the menorah was a symbol of God's light shining on the twelve tribes of Israel represented in the twelve loaves of bread placed on a table. The table sat across from the lampstand and each week the priests would replace the bread. Nearer to the curtain was a golden incense stand where fragrant smoke would rise up before God to create a pleasing aroma. It also acted as a smoke screen on the Day of Atonement for the high priest as he was instructed to create a cloud of incense over the mercy seat "or he will die" (Lev 16:13). We're not sure if the smoke hid the high priest or whether it blocked him from seeing God. In either case, the incense would save his life!

These different zones of holiness and the objects that reside in them are reflections of the wider universe. God dwells in the heavenly holy of holies and his glory radiates throughout the cosmos to varying degrees on the earth and in the waters below. This represents the threefold division of creation as it was understood in the ancient mind—heaven, earth, and the primordial waters beneath the earth, which often symbolized chaos. The tabernacle, in its threefold division, not only teaches the Israelites about the universal pattern of God's holiness, but it also teaches them how to approach him in worship. Drawing near to God in ancient Israel was not about singing a few songs, passing the offering plate, and then having a cup of coffee or tea. For Leviticus, approaching God was always an event where life and death hung in the balance. This is why it was so critical to follow his instructions and why Leviticus reminds us of what happens when those boundaries are transgressed.

THE KEEPERS OF THE CORE: PRIESTS AMONG A KINGDOM OF PRIESTS

Going back to our nuclear power plant image above, we can now begin to understand why God sets aside specific people for the task of worshipping and serving in the tabernacle. Priests in Leviticus are like highly skilled workers monitoring the core of the reactor to make sure that everything is safe. But safety in this instance comes by maintaining purity and holiness. Just as those working around the core of a nuclear reactor would go through training and particular rituals to ensure the safety of those around them, so too do the priests go through prescribed rituals to maintain the holiness of God's sanctuary.

The specific calling of humanity to care for God's home goes back to Genesis where we hear the priestly language in the command given to the first garden dwellers "to till it [the earth] and keep it" (Gen 2:15). The Hebrew verbs for "till" and "keep" can also be translated with the sense of "service/worship" and "guard/protect." The same words are often used to describe what the priests do in performing their duties in the sanctuary. In some ways, Adam and Eve functioned as the first "priests" in God's temple of Eden as those who care for, and protect, creation.

Priesthood is something that has existed from the beginning of the Bible and though it takes on different forms, it has always been a critical component of Israel's faith. This is because the priest performs a specific role and has a particular responsibility within the community of faith. For Adam and Eve that took place with the community of all creation but for the Israelites the priests function within the space of the tabernacle. In both cases, they are to perform their service by properly "keeping" the holy space where God dwells to benefit those around them. The priests in Leviticus are called to preserve God's order in creation by dividing between what is clean from what is unclean and preventing the chaos of sin from polluting God's sanctuary.

There are, however, common misconceptions about priesthood in contemporary Christian thinking. Some of this stems from current events that have bought to light tragic abuses committed by priests. Others conjure up stereotypes from historical traditions where priests were seen as the keepers of religious power. They have been viewed as the only ones holy enough to talk to God or lead others in worship and yet they are often seen as cold, aloof, and isolated within their own world, concealed by the walls of the church.

For those from Protestant traditions, priests can be also be seen as barriers to people coming to know Jesus in a personal faith and participating in the "priesthood of all believers." Priests are often viewed not as conduits to knowing God, but as obstacles for the true believer in experiencing the love and forgiveness of Christ.

Early Reformers were also concerned with priestly power over Scripture and its interpretation. They wanted to put the Bible back into the hands of ordinary people. The priests represented an elite class of religious figures in the church, often associated with the Pharisees and other Jewish religious leaders of the New Testament, that stood in the way of average believer engaging and learning from the scriptures.

No doubt all of these generalizations and stereotypes contain some elements of truth and history has proven that priests have not always been faithful to their calling. This should not, however, lead to the rejection of a specific role within the community of faith that was instituted by God. Instead, we can read Leviticus as the initial revelation for how priests were to function according to God's design as they served within his sacred space in order to bring blessing to the whole community.

The priests establish the worship of Israel to set the community apart from other nations that stand against the ways of God. They are given the responsibility to teach the people how to approach God in holiness so that they can discern between what is pure and impure. They preside within the sanctuary to make atonement for the people and to hold back the forces of chaos that threaten to destroy Israel and destroy the world. They are a visible sign of God's willingness to forgive, purify, and sanctify for the sake of his love for his people. When the priests do all these things they act as conduits of blessing, open channels that allow God's glory and favor to wash over his people.

Walter Brueggemann appropriately sums up the function of the original priesthood when he writes:

> While the temptation to a dualism that divides "life" from "worship" is real, it is important to see that worship models and enacts an alternative world of sanity that prevents Israel from succumbing to the seductive insanities of a world raging against the holiness of Yahweh the creator. The priesthood is to protect and guarantee the maintenance of this alternative world, wherein Israel could "see" God, and so see itself differently in the world.[3]

When we understand the original intent of God's commands concerning priests, we begin to see how this role was intended to bring life to the community of faith. Such a role was never fully realized in ancient Israel but was revealed and fulfilled through the great high priesthood of Christ.

3. Brueggemann, *Theology of the Old Testament*, 665.

And his priestly ministry continues today as it is lived out and made know through the church.

BRIDGE-BUILDERS

Before we discuss the ordination of Aaron and his sons in Leviticus (the first generation of priests in Israel), we need to see this event within the scope of God's vision for his people who are called to be a "kingdom of priests" (Exod 19:6). After the exodus from Egypt, the Israelites arrive at Mt. Sinai to enter into a covenant with God and to receive his teaching and commands. Before any instructions are given, however, God says to his people, "Now therefore, if you obey my voice and keep my covenant, you shall be my treasured possession out of all the peoples. Indeed, the whole earth is mine, but you shall be for me a priestly kingdom and a holy nation. These are the words that you shall speak to the Israelites" (Exod 19:5–6).

God sets aside one nation, the descendants of Abraham, out of all the nations of the world to be holy and to be a "kingdom of priests." The Israelites are not set apart because God cares less about the rest of the world. Instead he says "the whole earth is mine" to emphasize why he has called Israel to be his representatives on earth. A calling to a holy priesthood is placed on Israel *because* God loves all the nations and wants them to experience his salvation. The *exclusivity* of Israel is to serve the end goal of *inclusivity* for all peoples to experience God's redemption. So how were they meant to be a kingdom of priests?

In the ancient world the function of a priest was to intercede between the people and God. They brought sacrifices, offered prayers, and acted as a link between ordinary people and the divine. There is a Latin word that later became associated with the pope called *pontifex*. It was once used to refer to a class of priests in ancient Rome, but its origin comes from *pont-* "bridge" + *-fex* from the verb "make." The *pontifex* is a "bridge-builder," which offers an excellent visual for what Israel was called to do as a kingdom of priests. They were to be bridge-builders between humanity and God. By being obedient to God's commands and walking in holiness they would reflect his beauty, goodness, mercy, justice, and love to the surrounding nations. But if all of Israel was called to be a priestly and holy people, why was there a need for priests?

This is where we need to go back to our initial discussion of sacred space, graded holiness, and how a person can approach God. Only those with the proper training can enter the space that is closest to God's holiness. The priests were those trained with the specific task of making offerings for the people while also protecting them by preventing any unauthorized, and potentially lethal, contact with the holy. They were to ensure the highest level of purity in the sanctuary for the sake of the Israelites. Though they were separated from the community and held to a higher standard of purity, they became servants of the community by acting as conduits for God's blessing to flow out to his people.

The priests were also entrusted with the duty of teaching God's people how to live holy lives. They were charged with the command, "You must distinguish between the holy and the profane, and between the unclean and the clean; and you are to teach the people of Israel all the statutes that the LORD has spoken to them through Moses" (Lev 10:10–11). The priestly role was to preserve the purity of the tabernacle and to instruct people in the ways of purity. This was another critical aspect of maintaining holiness throughout all of Israel so that they would not profane God's tabernacle or the land.

When institutions fail and cause more harm than they do good, a common response is to want to get rid of the institution altogether. However, the institution of the priesthood in Israel was part of God's design. If the priests served humbly in their role, if they discerned between the sacred and the profane, if they taught about holiness and obeyed the commandments, they would provide a channel for God's grace to flow to the people.

When the priests functioned in their full capacity as bridge-builders, the floodgates of blessing would open and God would look favorably upon his people. This is summed up in the prayer that Aaron, the high priest, was instructed to say over all the Israelites.

> The LORD bless you and keep you;
> the LORD make his face to shine upon you and be gracious to you;
> the LORD lift up his countenance upon you and give you peace.
> So shall they put my name upon the people of Israel,
> and I will bless them. (Num 6:24–27)

This is the blessing of the priesthood when it functions as God intended. It's a system that sets apart some to serve for the benefit others by creating bridges to the divine for the people to experience his holy presence, his forgiveness, and his grace.

THE CONSECRATION OF AARON AND HIS SONS

The ordination of the first priests is found in Leviticus 8 and is linked to the previous instructions that Moses received in Exodus 29. One phrase that we hear repeated seven times in the chapter is that Moses was to do everything "as the LORD commanded." The emphasis on exact obedience highlights the volatility of the event. Like the scientist working in the innermost parts of the core reactor, life and death hangs in the balance of every precise movement and action.

The elaborate series of rituals begins with a washing. To consecrate anything as holy almost always requires purification by water. This became a more common practice around Jesus' day as the Jews developed all sorts of ritual baths in local communities and around the Jerusalem temple. John the Baptist offered his own ritual washing for repentance that preceded Jesus' ministry.

Aaron and his sons are washed and clothed in their priestly garments. Moses then takes the oil and anoints the different parts of the tabernacle and finishes by pouring the anointing oil upon Aaron's head. The symbolism is one of blessing and the overflow of God's grace to his people. We hear this in the words of the psalmist, who compares the harmony between God's people to be like "precious oil on the head, running down upon the beard, on the beard of Aaron, running down over the collar of his robes" (Ps 133:2). Aaron's life is now bound to the holiness of God's tabernacle.

After the animal sacrifices are performed, Moses takes a ram that is specifically offered for Aaron's consecration. He then takes some of the blood and puts it on Aaron's right earlobe, the thumb of his right hand, and the big toe of his right foot. He then does the same for Aaron's sons. The blood sprinkled on the altar is a sign of its cleansing and so too is the blood placed on the priests as of sign of their purification. Blood and oil are symbols that represent the purification of the person, literally from head to toe, as they transition from the profane and draw nearer to God's holiness.

The last step of ordination is to wait in a liminal state for seven days before they cross the threshold into God's sacred space. Their lives will then be permanently bound to the altar as they offer sacrifices on behalf of themselves and the community of faith. As they do, they keep at bay the forces of sin, impurity, and death. As Gorman writes, "The priesthood is established to stand at the intersection of chaos and order, pollution and purity, the holy and the profane."[4] The priests are the bridge-builders and play a key role in the institution of worship that God establishes in Israel. Their work is critical in ordering and maintaining the holiness of God's tabernacle and connecting the people to his presence.

---

4. Gorman, *The Ideology of Ritual Space*, 139.

ALIEN FIRE

The final precaution given to Aaron and his sons is to wait for the appointed period before they enter into the tabernacle, "So that you do not die" (Lev 8:35). The repeated warning of possible death highlights the critical need for absolute obedience and heightens the tension in the story as everything has been prepared exactly as God has commanded.

The consecration of the altar in Leviticus 9 is the next great climax in the story of God's salvation for his people. Once slaves in Egypt, delivered miraculously through plagues and the parting of the sea, given manna in the wilderness, and entering into covenant at Mt. Sinai, the act of consecrating the altar and establishing the worship of Israel will complete God's decent from the heavens to the earth. The altar is the place of atonement, purification, and the forgiveness of sin. Without sacrifice Israel would never be able to live in the presence of a holy God. And so Moses calls Aaron to "draw near" and "make atonement for yourself and for the people" (Lev 9:7).

After Aaron makes the inaugural sacrifices as the high priest the drama of the moment climaxes when "fire came out from the LORD'" and consumed the offering on the altar. The dramatic revelation is summed up in the people's response as "they shouted and fell on their faces" (v. 24). The tabernacle is now established as God's dwelling place on earth and his fire signifies his pleasure and acceptance of Israel's worship. The whole earth is full of God's glory but he has chosen to abide among his people in the tabernacle to bless them and to keep them and to make his face to shine upon them.

It's often the case in the Old Testament that when we reach a climactic moment of God's revelation, power, or grace it soon falls to pieces because of the peoples' disobedience. This happens in the wilderness, at Mt. Sinai, before going into the promised land, and on and on throughout Israel's history. Maybe the Old Testament authors knew that nothing can ever be perfect in the relationship between humanity and God. Rather than a depressing reality, however, the constant tension between God's holiness and human sin brings to light the Bible's emphasis on God's never-ending grace, mercy, patience, and compassion. The fact that God cares so much for his people, that he is willing to dwell with them *in spite of their disobedience*, and that he offers them a means for atonement, is truly the good news of salvation in the Old Testament.

Yet just when all is going well, when the world returns to its proper order, the entire scene is upended in just the first two verses of Leviticus 10.

> Now Aaron's sons, Nadab and Abihu, each took his censer, put fire in it, and laid incense on it; and they offered unholy fire

before the LORD, such as he had not commanded them. And fire came out from the presence of the LORD and consumed them, and they died before the LORD. (Lev 10:1–2)

The same holy fire that came down to consume the sacrifices as a sign of God's approval now breaks out to consume those who disobey God's command. We remember that in the previous two chapters we heard the constant refrain that everything was done "as the LORD commanded," but Aaron's sons do something that was "not commanded." Their actions are the equivalent of pushing the red self-destruct button in the inner core of the nuclear reactor. Not heeding God's word has disastrous consequences and, in this case, the consequence is death.

There has been a lot of debate about what Nadab and Abihu did that deserved the death penalty. The incense they used is called a "strange fire" or an "alien fire," which was unacceptable to God. It's likely that it wasn't so much the incense that they offered, but the fact that they did something that God had not commanded. Their actions demonstrate a sort of impudence and audacity in the holy place. It's as if they thought they could worship God on their own terms, without heeding his instructions.

There's also the possibility that the two were drunk while performing their duties since after the incident God tells Aaron that priests should not consume strong drink or wine when serving in the tabernacle (Lev 10:8–9). Whatever their sin, the phrase "alien fire" is probably best translated as "unauthorized fire" to highlight the consequences of disobedience to God's command.

The deaths of Nadab and Abihu are an illustration of what can happen to those who neither listen to God's word nor respect the power of his holiness. The story mentions nothing of God's wrath but focuses solely on how priests must behave as they draw near to his presence. Aaron's obedience results in blessing through God's divine fire of acceptance. Nadab and Abihu's disobedience results in death where divine fire becomes lethal.

We find a similar type of story in the New Testament that conveys the power of God's presence to be either life-giving or life-threatening. The scene of Ananias and Sapphira offers a warning to followers of Christ about what can happen if they lie to the community of faith (Acts 5:1–11). The couple had sold a piece of property and deceitfully withheld some of its proceeds as they pretended to give the full amount to the church. Peter confronts Ananias first and claims that his actions are the equivalent of lying to God. Upon being convicted, Ananias falls down dead and is buried. A few hours later the same fate befalls his wife Sapphira because they attempted to "test the Spirit of the Lord" (v. 9). The result was that a "great fear came upon the whole church" (v. 11) as new followers of Christ learned not to treat the power of the Holy Spirit with contempt.

Both stories punctuate the founding moments in the community of faith and act as warnings to inspire reverence and respect for the power of God's holiness. Were there other priests throughout Israel's history who disobeyed while serving in the tabernacle/temple who did not die? Probably. Were there other Christians who lied about their finances to the church who did not die? Almost certainly. These stories were not written to demonstrate how God responds to our disobedience in every instance. Instead, they serve as reminders that we worship a God who is loving, merciful, compassionate, and forgiving, but he is also awesome, holy, and "a consuming fire" (Heb 12:29).

THE INCARNATION: A NEW TEMPLE ON EARTH

The spatial and physical aspects of holiness are central to the entire book of Leviticus. With God's divine presence radiating from the holy of holies in the tabernacle, all of Israel must remain holy and approach his holiness with the utmost care and caution. To come into contact with his holiness in an inappropriate way could end in death. Yet drawing near to God in obedience to his command and with reverence leads to reconciliation, life, and the abundance of his blessing.

The rituals associated with the tabernacle were God's instructions to his people to teach them about who he is and how to worship him. The end goal was relationship and blessing. He would be their God and they would be his people. If Israel followed the commandments, they would grow in holiness and God would remain in their midst. The reality, however, is that the Old Testament recalls time and time again Israel's disobedience and failure to walk in his ways.

The prophets condemn the priests and people for ritual sacrifices that lack any meaning because they've neglected the moral and ethical commands to care for the poor and bring justice to the oppressed. Sacred space is defiled because of injustice, deceit, and wickedness. God said to the Israelites, "You shall not profane my holy name, that I may be sanctified among the people of Israel" (Lev 22:32), but the prophets, with one voice of rebuke, denounce the people for their inability to live as God's holy nation. The result is what Moses predicts in Leviticus 26; the land will be overtaken by the enemy, the sanctuary will be destroyed, and the people will be scattered into exile. This is what we witness in the Babylonian destruction of Jerusalem and the temple in 587 BCE.

The temple was rebuilt later under the leadership of Ezra and Nehemiah. This span of history, often called the Second Temple period, was a turbulent time in Jerusalem. Yet up until the first century AD, Jews continued to worship in the temple and the priests continued to offer their sacrifices.

Not all Jews accepted the legitimacy of the Jerusalem temple and others rejected the temple of Jesus' day, which was built by the maniacal Herod the Great. Yet the commands of Leviticus that had shaped Israel for centuries were maintained: sacrifice, purity laws, and rituals were practiced by Jews (and by Jesus himself) as a sign of God's holy presence in the temple of Jerusalem. But how did Jesus, as the Son of God, view himself in relationship to the temple?

The prologue to the Gospel of John offers one of the most profound claims of who Jesus is. "In the beginning was the Word, and the Word was with God, and the Word was God. He was in the beginning with God. All things came into being through him, and without him not one thing came into being" (John 1:1–3). As if this description is not breathtaking enough, the author goes on to say, "the Word became flesh and dwelt among us" (John 1:14). Any Jew reading this in the original language might have been unsettled by John's use of "dwelt." The word could be translated as "tabernacled" since it's the same word used in the Greek translation of the Old Testament to describe God's glory and holiness dwelling in the tabernacle. The allusion is crystal clear—Jesus is the fullness of God's divine presence *in the flesh*. This is further confirmed in John 2 when Jesus claims he will destroy the temple and rebuild it in three days but he was "speaking of the temple *of his body*" (John 2:21). The glory that once resided in the holy of holies now resides in the man, Jesus.

The incarnation, God's tabernacling glory in Jesus, is the beginning of a new era in salvation. Just as God came down to dwell in the midst of his people to bring liberation, reconciliation, and blessing, so too does he come down again, but this time it's in a living, breathing, human being. If Jesus is the fullness of God's glory in the flesh, then how does he treat the instructions in Leviticus about holiness, purity, and sacrifice in relation to the temple?

There is not enough space to survey all of the Gospels, but we might look at a few episodes from the Gospel of Mark. In doing so we'll see that there are times that Jesus upholds the commands of Leviticus. At other times his actions or teachings conflict with Leviticus, and at other points he demonstrates that he surpasses Leviticus because of his holiness as the Son of God.

We don't have to go far in Mark's Gospel before we see Jesus' actions conflicting with the requirements of Leviticus. A significant aspect of the tabernacle/temple was that it was the only place where sacrifices could be made to atone for sin. After the healing of a leper Jesus then encounters a paralytic (Mark 2:1–12). He says to the man, "My son, your sins are forgiven," and those listening rightfully accuse him in their inner thoughts of blaspheming God's name. Who can forgive sins except God alone and how can sins be forgiven except through obedience to the Levitical commands concerning sacrifice and blood shed on the altar?

Here Jesus places himself above the commandments because the power to forgive sin, which was once confined to rituals performed in the temple, is now present in the flesh. Jesus is the atoning presence of God and we witness the visual power of forgiveness as the paralytic rises from his mat to full restoration.

In the following chapter of Mark the themes of wholeness, healing, and restoration are taken up again when Jesus confronts the Jewish leaders about what is appropriate for the Sabbath. We will speak more about the Sabbath in chapter 5, but the command for rest on the seventh day is central to the teachings of Leviticus. The Sabbath is a gift and a sign of the rest and refreshment that God desires for his people. The Sabbath is also a movement toward wholeness on all levels of society whether it be social, political, or economic.[5] And so Jesus, seeing a man with a withered hand, asks the religious leaders, "Is it lawful to do good or to do harm on the Sabbath, to save life or to kill" (Mark 3:4). When he heals the man he is not rejecting the Old Testament command but, rather, he is fulfilling God's original intention for the Sabbath as a day to do good, to save life, and to bring about the fullness of his restoration.

As the gospel narrative continues, Jesus encounters a woman who has experienced bleeding for twelve years (Mark 5:25–34). Certain types of blood discharge were signs of impurity in Leviticus, which meant separation from the community and the tabernacle. The length of time this woman had been bleeding reminds us that she had been banned from approaching the temple in Jerusalem for a significant portion of her life. Such alienation from God and the stigma of uncleanness in her community had led her to spend everything she had on doctors, but nothing helped (5:26). In desperation she reached out among the throngs to touch Jesus' clothes and she was immediately healed (5:29). Jesus turns to her and says, "Daughter, your faith has made you well; go in peace, and be healed of your disease" (5:34). We've already been told that she was healed immediately, but Jesus seems to be speaking on another level of wholeness. Not only has she been healed physically of her bleeding, she has been healed through her purification by being restored to the community of faith and by being reconciled to God.

---

5. See Scarlata, *Sabbath Rest*.

We know from Leviticus 12 that a woman in menstruation, or bleeding after childbirth, was ritually unclean, but rather than being defiled by contact with her impurity, Jesus' power once again brings healing. Any normal person would've become unclean by this encounter, but the gospel writer reminds us that Jesus is not a "normal" person. He is filled with the holiness of God that can heal, cleanse, and restore to life.

Following this, Jesus arrives at Jairus' home only to be told that his daughter is dead. To touch a dead human or animal resulted in immediate impurity, according to Leviticus 21:1–11, yet Jesus takes the girl's hand and she is restored to life (Mark 5:35–43). Even the power of death cannot hinder the holiness and healing of God's presence in Christ.

Jesus also teaches his disciples about the kingdom of God and the new reality of holiness in the light of his presence on earth. In Mark 7:14–23 Jesus tells the people that a person cannot be defiled by what goes into their bodies, but impurity comes from the evil that resides in the heart. The gospel writer then explains that Jesus "declared all foods clean" (7:19). This is possibly the clearest example of Jesus' teaching standing in direct opposition to the instructions given to Moses about what Israel is permitted to eat in order to maintain their purity. We'll discuss the food regulations of Leviticus 11 in the next chapter, but Israel's strict dietary requirements were a critical sign of what set them apart as God's chosen people. Is Jesus forsaking the commands given in Leviticus to start some new religion based on his own teaching? This may seem confusing because on other occasions, as we'll see, Jesus clearly upholds the laws of Leviticus in loving one's neighbor, being obedient to the Sabbath, or instructing lepers to be examined by the priests. Why then does he seemingly dismiss the food laws?

In this instance, the divine holiness of Christ clearly surpasses particular commands of the first covenant, but we should not be too quick to dismiss the dietary rules completely. We recall in the Sermon on the Mount that Jesus says, "Do not think that I have come to abolish the law or the prophets; I have come not to abolish but to fulfill" (Matt 5:17). There is a critical interpretive distinction between "abolish" and "fulfill." Jesus does not abolish the dietary regulations of Leviticus, but he does fulfill them. Restrictions on food were given to instruct Israel on purity *in relation to the tabernacle*. However, with God's holiness revealed in Christ, those restrictions no longer apply. What once defiled Israel in relation to the tabernacle does so no more because a revelation greater than the tabernacle has come.

Let's look at one last example where Jesus lashes out at those in the Jerusalem temple for perverting the sacrificial offerings commanded in Leviticus. Often called the "cleansing of the temple," Jesus enters the outer court of Herod's Temple, which was known as the court of the gentiles. This addition to the Temple Mount was not a part of the original instructions given by God to Moses. The court was created by Herod because he was only half-Jewish and would not have been able to enter into the temple otherwise. This area was open to all foreigners and females and was a busy area of commerce.

The gentile court was where people coming to the temple could purchase animals for sacrifices. Oftentimes pilgrims would travel long distances to reach Jerusalem and could not bring animals with them. Instead, they brought money from their own lands, which would need to be converted at the temple. You can quickly get the picture of money changers using dishonest weights and cheating people in their exchanges. We can also imagine others selling animals that were lame or second-rate and not the required unblemished sacrifices Leviticus prescribes.

Traders would likely have had shifting prices, depending on demand, which would have made it impossible for poorer people to purchase animals or birds. In fact, in a collection of early Jewish writings called the Mishna, the rabbis lamented the fact that pigeons (a sacrifice offered by those who were poor) were being sold at exorbitant prices. The temple was meant to be the most holy place of God's presence, but it had been desecrated by injustice, cheating, and dishonest gain. The whole scene might be summed up as the act of profaning God's name or, in other words, making a mockery of the power of his holiness.

Jesus responds by creating no small amount of chaos when he overturns the money changers' tables and drives out the animals with a whip, according to John's account (John 2:13–17). Jesus then refers to the prophets Isaiah and Jeremiah by declaring, "Is it not written, 'My house shall be called a house of prayer for all the nations'? But you have made it a den of robbers" (Mark 11:17). The Scriptures convey God's intent for the temple as a sign of his presence and a place for worship, prayer, and sacrifice for anyone who draws near to him.

What is so striking in Jesus' actions is not the dramatic outburst of anger but the fact that he is upholding the same standards that Leviticus places on sacred space and the need to maintain its purity. Jesus upholds the sanctity of the temple space and, like the prophet Zechariah, looks forward to a time when "there shall no longer be traders in the house of the LORD of hosts on that day" (Zech 14:21). This prophetic act of symbolically purifying the temple may have been a deliberate foreshadowing of the purification that was to come through Jesus' death and resurrection. It may also have pointed to the final destruction of the temple by the Romans in 70 AD. However we interpret Jesus' actions, we see his recognition of sacred space in the temple as God had commanded in Leviticus. Though he himself reflects the fullness of God's glory, Jesus demonstrates his zeal for God's house to be a holy site where all nations are welcomed to worship.

This brief look at the Gospel of Mark highlights how critical it is to understand the life and ministry of Jesus in the light of Leviticus and its standards for holiness, purity, and sacred space. Jesus is the tabernacling presence of God in the flesh who fulfills the Old Testament commands and opens up the way for creating a new temple on earth—the body of Christ.

THE GREAT HIGH PRIEST AND A LIVING TEMPLE

The priesthood, sacred space, and atonement, which were so critical in instructing the ancient Israelites in the life of faith, do not end after the death, resurrection, and ascension of Christ. In fact, the entire epistle written to the Hebrews is the longest defense in the New Testament of how Jewish followers of Christ could relate to Jesus as the one, true, great high priest.

We cannot survey the entire Epistle to the Hebrews, but one significant issue in understanding Jesus as a priestly figure is that he doesn't have the right lineage. We know that Jesus is from the tribe of Judah, a *royal* line, and is often referred to in the Gospels as the "Son of David." However, God is very clear in Leviticus and throughout the Old Testament that priests should come from the tribe of *Levi* (though there seem to be some exceptions).

Instead of trying to shoehorn Jesus into the priestly line, the author of Hebrews ties Jesus' priesthood to that of a mysterious figure who appears once in Genesis (14:18). He is called Melchizedek and he is the priest-king of "Salem" (likely referring to Jerusalem). This priest-king has no genealogy given in the text, with "neither beginning of days nor end of life" (Heb 7:3), and yet God made him both priest and king. With the dawn of the new covenant, Jesus has ascended into the heavens and has surpassed Melchizedek by becoming the eternal high priest who resides in the true holy of holies with the Father and the Spirit (Heb 7:1—9:28).

One of the most significant distinctions, however, between Jesus and Melchizedek (or even the angels) is that he was one of us—fully human and capable of suffering. The author writes, "For we do not have a high priest who is unable to sympathize with our weaknesses, but we have one who in every respect has been tested as we are, yet without sin" (Heb 4:15). Jesus is the only one able to become the high priest of all humanity because he has suffered as we suffer, he understands our pain, and can empathize with our weakness (Heb 5:1–10).

The sacrifices of Israel's high priests occurred every year for the forgiveness of sin, but Christ offers himself *once for all* on the cross. "For by a single offering he has perfected for all time those who are sanctified" (Heb 10:14). By this one sacrifice, Christ has not only entered into the true holy of holies in the heavenly realms, where he intercedes for us, but he has also invited us to draw near to God's holiness. In what feels like the high point of the letter to the Hebrews, the author's arguments about Jesus as the great high priest culminate as he writes:

> Therefore, my friends, since we have confidence to enter the sanctuary by the blood of Jesus, by the new and living way that he opened for us through the curtain (that is, through his flesh), and since we have a great priest over the house of God, let us approach with a true heart in full assurance of faith, with our hearts sprinkled clean from an evil conscience and our bodies washed with pure water. (Heb 10:19–22)

The fingerprints of Leviticus cover this remarkable statement of faith. The blood of Christ, the atoning sacrifice at God's altar, has allowed us impure human beings to enter through that curtain (*parokhet*) embroidered with cherubim guarding the way to the holy of holies in the tabernacle. This new reality is symbolized in Matthew and Mark's Gospels at the crucifixion when the temple curtain is torn in two (Matt 27:51; Mark 15:38). The place once reserved for the high priest alone has been opened through Christ's broken body on the cross now represented in the broken bread of the Eucharist. Jesus has become the perfect, eternal high priest who is the ultimate bridge-builder between God and humanity and he has invited us to enter into God's presence through his sacrifice.

We also note the allusion to the sprinkling of blood as the believer's heart is "sprinkled clean" (cf. Exod 24.8). We're reminded that only *objects* in the tabernacle (and priests and lepers) were ever anointed with blood in Leviticus. Yet like all of these objects transitioning into a further state of holiness, so too are we drawing nearer to God's holiness through the offering and priesthood of Christ.

In some churches today there is little, if any, emphasis on Christ as the great high priest who continues in his ministry by interceding for us at the right hand of the Father (Heb 7:23–25). If Christians do acknowledge Christ as priest, sometimes they simply reduce his role to a personal intercessor. But Christ the heavenly high priest continues to intercede and maintain his priestly duty over the temple he is building on earth—the body of Christ, the church.

The apostle Paul speaks of a dividing wall that has come down between Jew and gentile so that now all stand together as "fellow citizens" in the household of God. The community of believers is being built up on the cornerstone of Christ and is bound together in him and "grows into a holy temple in the Lord" (Eph 2:21).

The apostle Peter uses similar temple language to describe the new church of Christ when he refers to the believers as "living stones." He encourages them to "be built into a spiritual house, to be a holy priesthood, to offer spiritual sacrifices acceptable to God through Jesus Christ" (1 Pet 2:5).

In the New Testament, the church becomes the dwelling place of God's holiness in the form of the Holy Spirit inhabiting his people. No longer bound by geographical location, the Spirit of God abides wherever his people gather together in Christ. The new temple that brings together all humanity, united in Christ, is a global temple presided over by Jesus, the living, eternal high priest. God did not institute the tabernacle and priesthood centuries earlier to have it disappear once Jesus came. Instead, Jesus fills out the full measure and glory of what it means to have a perfect high priest who has offered the perfect sacrifice and now intercedes for his church, the new temple on earth.

SACRED SPACE TODAY

The world is no less filled with the glory of God today than it was in ancient Israel. The problem in recognizing sacred space is not with creation, but with *us*. Our desacralization of our surroundings has left us in a profane world that no longer has room for the sacred. If we think that by "proving" how the world works we can somehow strip it of its mystery or divine presence, then we have missed what Leviticus teaches us about God and a life of holiness. His holy presence abided on earth in his tabernacle/temple and extended outwards to the covenant people and to the land. This was the locus of salvation for Israel and for all the nations. But a new revelation has come through Christ, the tabernacling presence of God's holiness. Through his death, resurrection, and ascension to become both Lord and high priest, he is made known by the presence of the Holy Spirit in the gathered church throughout the world.

The presence of God's holiness continues to be mediated by the spaces we inhabit. Churches, buildings, gardens, forests, or mountains can all be sacred when we become conscious of God's presence in them. If we gain any understanding from the worldview of Leviticus, we recognize that God has consecrated all things, including the spaces we inhabit. Nothing is beyond his holy presence.

We also learn from Leviticus that not all places are equally holy. Though we no longer need to divide the world into the sacred and profane, because Christ's holiness fills all creation, we do experience that holiness in different measures in different places. Maybe you've had the experience of entering a holy site or an ancient church where the prayers of the faithful have been offered for centuries and you feel something different in that place. It could be visiting the land where Jesus walked, cathedrals, or places marked by the lives of the saints. In these sites we sense a sacred heritage that has built up over the centuries that we too can now witness.

To experience the world as sacramental in a desacralized culture requires us to rethink how we experience God's holiness in the world. It calls for a reassessment of our encounters with the holy as we go through our days. This may be in specific places, or the people we meet, or the work we set out to do. In each instance we see God in all things, which means that all things are being consecrated in Christ and moving toward holiness.[6]

Imagine if you were born with a condition that caused you to see the world in black and white. Now imagine that a doctor gave you a pair of prescription lenses that meant you could see the world in its fullest, most vivid and vibrant colors. Looking through those lenses is like seeing through the eyes of Leviticus where all the world is radiating with God's holiness. The world has meaning and every creature has value because God is fully present in the world. This sacramental approach to life is eloquently expressed by Elizabeth Barrett Browning in her poem *Aurora Leigh*.

> Earth's crammed with heaven,
> And every common bush afire with God;
> But only he who sees takes off his shoes,
> The rest sit round and pluck blackberries,
> And daub their natural faces unaware
> More and more from the first similitude.[7]

Many of us are like those sitting around picking blackberries, completely unaware of Christ's presence in our midst. Whether it's in physical buildings, natural places, or where two or more are gathered in his name, our world is "crammed with heaven" waiting for us to bear witness, to take off our shoes, and worship because we are standing on holy ground.

---

6. See Brown, *God and Enchantment of Space*.
7. Elizabeth Barrett Browning, *Aurora Leigh*, 246 (lines 821–26).

4

You Are What You Eat

Food, Faithfulness, and Family

FOOD AND FAITH

Our next stop takes us beyond the world of the tabernacle and into the average Israelite home where everyday rituals become signs and reminders of God's presence and Israel's call to be holy. Not only do food and purity laws remind Israel of their identity as God's chosen people, but they also remind them of how they are to live in relationship with creation. Though some of the restrictions around food and family might seem incredibly odd to the modern reader of Leviticus, they are, perhaps, some of the most important in reminding Christians what it means to offer one's whole life to God and how to live within the community of creation.

One of the themes that we've picked up on so far in Leviticus is that living in proximity to God's presence requires that every part of one's life be consecrated as holy. If his holiness resides in the tabernacle and radiates outward into the community, then everything around his dwelling place must also be holy. This means that even the simplest and most basic acts of daily life, like eating and drinking, must reflect his purity.

Leviticus gives us a vision of whole-life discipleship. If God's people are to be a kingdom of priests and a holy nation, then everything they do becomes a sign of faithfulness to God's command. This is why when we turn to Leviticus 11 we discover the most extensive food regulations in the Bible. The restrictions don't offer a summary of everything the Israelites can or cannot eat, but they provide a framework for the people to distinguish between things that are pure and impure.

We have discussed the power that rituals have on how we learn and gain knowledge about God. Rituals are outward, embodied actions that express and help shape our inward beliefs. In chapter 2 we looked at the rituals around sacrifice at the altar, but now we see how rituals are to be established in the home on a daily basis. These patterns in everyday life within the family are meant to bring about further knowledge of God's holiness and Israel's call to be a holy people.

The prescriptions regarding food have had such a profound impact on shaping the life and faith of God's people that thousands of years later they are still practiced by many Jews today. The rules of *kashrut,* or kosher laws, have grown over the centuries but they are still founded on the basic principles of Leviticus.

Food is the most basic necessity of life and what better way to remember who you are by linking it to what you eat. The old saying "you are what you eat" is particularly true in the case of ancient Israel. Every time they sat down to eat they had to think about whether or not what they put in their mouth would make them unclean in relation to the tabernacle. Each bite reminded them that they were God's chosen people, separated, called to purity, holiness, and obedience to his commands. Within this framework, the act of eating becomes a ritual that shapes identity. Food becomes a sign not only of God's physical provision, but of each person's spiritual formation.

In the industrialized, developed world we easily forget how central the act of eating is to life. We take it for granted that we can pop round the local shops and pick up something any time of day. Meat is prepared for us, vegetables are pre-washed and sliced, sandwiches are made and boxed for easy eating on the go. We don't often consider where the food has come from or what's in it. Lengthy ingredient lists are often scrawled on packages in microscopic print along with the place of origin, which may have been a country thousands of miles away. We don't know how the food has been produced, how it has been transported, how it has been processed, and, for the most part, we don't care. We've become so accustomed to knowing virtually nothing about food production that eating becomes a mindless, physical act with the end goal of simply satisfying our appetites.

God, however, intended food to be something more than just physical sustenance for our bodies. Moses reminds the Israelites of this when they are on the verge of entering into the promised land. He recalls God's provision of manna, the bread from heaven that Israel ate while wandering through the wilderness. He tells them that this was not given only for the sake of their physical nourishment, but in order to teach them that "one does not live by bread alone, but by every word that comes from the mouth of the LORD" (Deut 8:3). Manna was a gift and a sign of God's provision for the body, but it was also a reminder that true life comes from obedience to God's word. Even before entering into covenant with God when Israel wandered toward Mt. Sinai, they were being taught to make connections between food and faith.

The link between eating and spirituality can have profound consequences on how we live our lives. To put this in a more modern context, we might think about a person who is morally committed to a vegan lifestyle. For a vegan, food is an important part of their identity. They are dedicated to abstaining from anything that has come from an animal and refuse to eat meat, seafood, or dairy products. Lists of what can or cannot be eaten might change slightly between vegans but at the heart of their belief is that it's unethical to eat anything that comes from the animal kingdom.

Some vegans also move beyond food to apply the same principle to other aspects of life. They may choose not to wear clothing made of fur, leather, down, or wool because it comes from animals. They might not purchase items such as cosmetics that were developed by using animals in their testing process. They might even refuse to go to the zoo or to places where animals are used for entertainment or sport. Their ethical beliefs shape their identity and their actions.

To be a vegan in the developed world requires a lot of forethought, especially when it comes to eating. Every time you go to a grocery store or to a restaurant you need to consider what you are purchasing and where it comes from. If you went to a friend's house it might mean not eating certain things that were prepared. You might have to carry food with you in some instances so that you wouldn't have to compromise your beliefs. Every time food is placed before you, every time you get hungry, or when you go out with friends you are reminded of who you are and who you profess to be.

The dietary regulations of Leviticus achieve a similar goal. They are God's way of establishing food rituals in the life of his people that will act as constant reminders of who they are and who they are called to be. When food is bound up with the life of faith the simple act of eating becomes an expression of obedience, witness, and identity-formation. All human beings must eat but when the act of consuming is linked to God's command, we submit our most essential appetites to the pursuit of holiness. Israel was called to be a holy people and by restricting their consumption they were constantly reminded of their call to purity, holiness, and their place within the community of God's creation.

What was the reason for establishing dietary regulations? God never gave anyone in Genesis rules for eating (apart from not consuming blood), so why start now? We remember that everything in Leviticus stands in relation to the new reality of God's permanent presence residing in the tabernacle. Because God's holiness now dwells on earth a new relationship within the covenant must be established. It's not that God has changed since Genesis, but the circumstances of his salvation on the earth have been revealed.[1] The light of his holiness and purity have come to inhabit the world and his people must order their lives according to that holiness, even by how they eat.

EATING OUR WAY TO HOLINESS

The detail and repetition of Leviticus 11 is enough to drive the modern reader to despair. How often can we read about animals that have cloven hoofs and do, or do not, chew the cud? And how many types of birds, locusts, or lizards can we read about without feeling like we've been plunged into a *National Geographic* nature program? The lists of creatures are not exhaustive, but they provide enough detail of local species to make us scratch our heads when we begin to think about why some are singled out and others are not, especially the rock badger!

There are no explanations for why certain animals should be considered clean or unclean. Leviticus presumes that the reader understands why some creatures are permitted to be eaten, but it never offers a rational reason. There have been attempts to find logical patterns behind the dietary laws. Some have argued that they were given to promote good hygiene, which might be true in some instances but not in others. Another argument is that the food restrictions had to do with Israel distinguishing itself from its gentile neighbors, like the Philistines who we know did raise pigs for food. This may explain the ban on eating pork, but it doesn't offer answers for other prohibitions.

The most comprehensive approach to the dietary laws is offered by anthropologist Mary Douglas in her classic book *Purity and Danger*. In it she describes how cultures apply symbolic meaning to different rituals that don't often follow the patterns of modern pragmatism. Instead, they form an inner logic that reflects the symbols and beliefs of that culture. In Israelite culture what you eat becomes tied to larger systems of belief that reflect the

---

1. We also note that the original human diet was plant-based as explained in Gen 1:29. There was, therefore, no need for food restrictions until after the exile from Eden.

character and wisdom of God. If God is just, merciful, loving, and protects the most vulnerable, then the way we eat should reflect that same character.

Douglas sees three major divisions in the dietary code; creatures in the *air*, creatures on *land*, and creatures in the *water*.[2] Within each category the Israelites are told what they can and cannot eat, but each group seems to have its own guiding principles. For land animals there is an emphasis on cloven hoofs and chewing the cud. If an animal has cloven hoofs and chews the cud, they're clean and can be eaten. But if it chews the cud and does not have a cloven hoof, then it's unclean. This is why the Israelites can't eat rock badgers. It makes perfect sense!

In the waters the guiding principle is that anything with fins and scales can be eaten. Douglas thinks that, in this instance, what is at stake is locomotion and how a creature naturally moves in the water. Things that "walk" along the seafloor (walking is for land animals) are unclean for Israel because they don't follow the typical manner of creatures swimming in the water. The symbol of natural movement in land, air, or sea becomes a sign of purity and impurity.

The same might be true for insects (Lev 11:20–23). Insects with wings that "walk" are not to be eaten, but if they have joint legs and hop then they're fine. Locusts and crickets fall into the clean category while other insects do not. I'm not sure what other insects anyone would want to eat, but if you fancied a grilled locust then you could at least remain ritually pure.

When it comes to the birds of the air there may be ethical reasons attached to what you can or cannot eat. Several of the birds listed in Leviticus, like the eagle, the vulture, and the owl, are birds of prey. If caring for the poor and vulnerable is at the heart of God's commandments, then the Israelites should not consume any species that preys on weaker creatures. It's as if consuming a bird of prey would somehow increase your own aggression toward others which may lead to unethical behavior or acts of violence.

Some of the earliest rabbinic interpretations of Leviticus saw these dietary laws as a means to enforce ideas of social justice that would lead to holiness. By abstaining from violent, predatory creatures one could cultivate their own character by growing toward a life of non-violence.

The last major category is the "swarming things," which describes different species of animals and lizards (Lev 11:29–31, 41–43). The prohibitions here may have to do with fertility as we recall the "swarming things" that God creates in Genesis 1 were commanded to "be fruitful and multiply." To eat them might be sign of going against God's original design or somehow limiting their fertility.

---

2. Douglas, *Purity and Danger*, 56–57.

These different theories may or may not explain the exact meaning behind some of these dietary restrictions. What is important for us as readers today is to question what the commands were trying to achieve in the life of God's people. We might not discover all the answers, but we can be sure that *eating relates to holiness*. What we put into our mouths represents what we believe in our hearts. At the end of all the dietary commands God reminds the people, "For I am the LORD your God; sanctify yourselves therefore, and be holy, for I am holy" (Lev 11:44). Somehow these seemingly random classifications of birds, animals, reptiles, and insects relates to Israel's purity and holiness.

The dietary code found in Leviticus might seem completely illogical to the modern reader. But when we step back for a moment and look at the end goal of the dietary restrictions we find that there are valuable lessons for us to learn about God and how we live in holiness as we consider our role within creation. 1) Limiting our diets to certain types of animals that God prescribes helps instill a reverence for all life. We do not blindly consume any creature we desire but we restrict ourselves as a sign of obedience to God and our care for creation. 2) Submitting our physical appetites and consumption to God demonstrates that we are willing to offer him both our physical and spiritual lives in the pursuit of holiness. 3) Restraining from certain foods teaches us humility as we acknowledge that God is the giver of all life and only he can dictate what can or cannot be eaten. 4) Finally, the food we eat becomes a sign of worship and holiness. Eating is not just for physical sustenance, but it becomes a way in which we celebrate our relationship with God and the rest of creation.

"DETESTABLE" FOOD AND THE DIET OF ANCIENT ISRAEL

If you're an animal-lover or naturalist it might be difficult to listen to the language of Leviticus 11 when it names certain things in God's creation as "detestable" or an "abomination." When God created the world in Genesis he declared everything to be good, even very good. How could God's good creation all of a sudden become detestable for his people?

Once again, we need to remember the context of Leviticus and this particular point in Israel's history. We're no longer in the world of Eden where God's holiness filled all creation and he dwelt in the fullness of his presence with his children. In the books of Exodus and Leviticus God is entering into a sinful, broken world in need of his healing and wholeness. But to enter into our space-time where sin and death exist, God defines new boundaries and categories for how humanity might live in the presence of his holiness. Creatures that are now "detestable" to Israel are not any less a part of God's good creation. Instead, the emphasis is on how eating these creatures makes Israel ritually unclean in relation to the purity of the tabernacle. The concern of Leviticus is maintaining the purity of the people through what they eat so that God's dwelling place is not defiled.

Part of the challenge of these verses is how the words "abomination" and "detestable" are translated in English. The Hebrew noun (*sheqets*) is almost exclusively used in Leviticus 11 and might be more accurately rendered with the sense of something that is to be *completely banned* or rejected. When we read that certain creatures are, "detestable to you . . ." (Lev 11:10), we can interpret this as something that Israel should "completely ban" from their diets. The command is *not* a commentary on the goodness of the creatures themselves but, rather, on the potential they have to make Israel impure in relation to the tabernacle.

It does not make sense to think that God suddenly considers camels, whales, ostriches, or rock badgers to be an abomination. God is the one who brought into being all of creation in order for it to exist in a complex, interdependent ecosystem that relies on the participation of every living thing. The gecko, the locust, the tawny owl, or the simple hare all contribute to the vast, interconnected network of life. They are all beautiful works of the Creator's hands, but in the worshipping life of his people they are to be completely banned from consumption.

Having considered foods that were prohibited, we might think for a moment about the ancient Israelite household and what they could eat. Ancient Israelite farms were small ecosystems that relied on the work of each family member and animal to sustain its production of food and other products. In subsistence farming there is no room for waste since the margins of gain were slim or in some seasons non-existent. If there was not enough rain or if a family could not afford seed, they would go through "hungry seasons" where there was very little to eat.

Archeologist Baruch Rosen calculates that the average Israelite subsistence farmer would experience a shortfall of about fifteen million calories per year.[3] This meant that the average family would experience food shortages for approximately sixty days a year. We remember God's command to leave the edges of one's fields unharvested so that the poor could glean from them (Lev 19:6). This was not giving out of one's abundance but, rather, it was sacrificing one's essential food supply for the sake of caring for the poor.

---

3. Rosen, "Subsistence Economy," 348–49.

Care for the land was critical and farmers practiced crop rotation to maintain the soil's fertility. Leaving fields fallow for a time helped them recover natural minerals and nutrients. Unseeded fields were excellent pastures for livestock who in turn left their natural deposits of manure, which nourished the soil. Animals also helped aerate the land as they walked through the fields. This allowed for the soil to recover its nutrients and serve as fertile ground for future crops.

Unlike other parts of the world, Israel was reliant mainly on the summer and winter rains. The majority of precipitation came between late October and late April. Without nearby natural springs, the Israelites constructed massive cisterns underground to collect the runoff and to provide water during the dry season. There were no vast systems of irrigation for their crops like in Egypt or parts of Mesopotamia. This added yet another layer of instability to their lives. If there was no rain there would be famine, but if there was too much rain the crops might also be destroyed. Israel's home is described as "a land flowing with milk and honey" in the Old Testament, but the realities of life could often prove the opposite.

Much of the land in Israel is rocky and hilly, which led the Israelites to create terraced fields like their gentile neighbors. Digging into the rocky soil and creating walled beds along the slopes was the best way to capture rain for the crops. Excess water could trickle down the hills slowly to prevent flooding or erosion while also saturating the soil. Terraced farming is labor-intensive but offered a stable system of managing crops for Israelite families. This allowed them to be self-sufficient and to produce enough for their own needs, but little, if any, for trade in the marketplace.[4]

In addition to agriculture, animal husbandry was critical to the life of the family. The most common livestock in Israel were goats and sheep. These provided wool for textiles, milk, cheese, fat for candles, and skins for holding water or wine. They also offered the main source of meat in the Israelite diet, which for many was rare apart from festivals or special occasions. Cattle and oxen were more valuable and played a critical role in the life of the farm. These animals took on a massive workload in plowing the fields or treading out the grain from the harvest. They were far too valuable to eat for the common person, so when Leviticus talks about killing a calf or bull at the altar this was a *monumental* sacrifice for most people. If we translated this into modern terms, it might be like bringing your car to church and offering it as a gift. For many in the West, cars are an essential part of life and it would be an enormous sacrifice to give it up.

---

4. Meyers, *Rediscovering Eve*, 45–47.

The other important point about animals is that they were essentially like members of the family. In some Israelite dwellings the animals shared a room of the house. These were not pets that had no particular function but, rather, they were instrumental to the household and contributed to its survival. The command for animals to share in Sabbath rest each week was a reminder to the Israelites that they were to treat their livestock with compassion. God would not allow a nation once yoked in slavery to turn around and impose the same bondage on their animals.

Leviticus is clear that animals on the farm were to be treated with dignity and justice. This sentiment is echoed in Deuteronomy where God gives the command, "You shall not muzzle an ox while it is treading out the grain" (Deut 25:4), which we saw was quoted by Paul (1 Cor 9:10-12). As oxen walk over the grain to help extract the kernels, they can eat a significant amount over the course of a day. To bind their mouths while they work would be unjust and cruel. Even if it meant sacrificing some of the grain that would go toward sustaining the family, the Israelites were commanded to allow their animals a fair share of food from their labor.

It's no wonder that the slaughter of domestic animals in Leviticus is treated as a sacred event that only takes place at the altar (Lev 17:3-5). A later Jewish collection of rabbinic laws (called the Talmud) states that the method of slaughter should be humane. This was to cultivate a sensitivity to the magnitude of handling life, death, and blood in the presence of God.

It does not take much to realize that animal care in ancient Israel is a far cry from the industrialized factory farms that breed and slaughter animals today. Rather than being integral to the family and the environment, animals are often raised in severely constrained conditions. Cattle, pigs, and chickens are confined to metal-barred pens where they live nearly all their life eating artificial feed that is mixed with a combination of growth hormones and antibiotics to prevent disease. These animals are forced to stand in their own excrement, if they can stand at all. Oftentimes their bodies develop so rapidly and disproportionately that they cannot support themselves any longer. All of this takes place behind factory walls and barbed-wire fences away from public view. Many of these animals will not see daylight their entire lives.

Then there is the process of mass slaughter, which occurs in factory-line style. In many instances animals are stressed from the pre-slaughter process of being driven, shocked, and prodded through metal gates. Stun guns fired into a cow's forehead are not always successful and sometimes they are butchered by machinery while still alive. The process is graphic but important to understand for anyone who consumes meat. I won't go into further detail here, but a simple search online for industrial slaughter will offer more than one cares to see.

Not all slaughterhouses are inhumane or cruel to animals. Some demonstrate respect for life and the sacredness of creation. This is happening in some large-scale slaughterhouses but also in many small-share farms that strive for an ecological balance between their crops and animals. Thankfully these agricultural enterprises are springing up more and more in the West, but like any farm, they are in need of consumer support.

Though we may often go to the market or the grocery store in search of the lowest prices, Leviticus reminds us that our consumer conscience should also consider where our food has come from, how it has been raised, and how those who produced it have been treated. We, the consumers, are culpable when we blindly participate in a global agricultural system that treats living beings as a commodity to be sold for profit. Israel was bound by God's command to treat all life as sacred in order to maintain the holiness of the covenant community. The church must also take on that role for the sake of preserving the holiness of Christ throughout the world.

When we consider the diet of the ancient Israelites, meat was not a typical source of nutrition. The main staples of the Mediterranean diet were grains, wine, and oil. The grains (mainly barley and wheat) were the most important and made up the bulk of daily calories. The word for "bread" (*leḥem*) is often used in Scripture as a term for food in general. Bread was the core food of life and was produced through a laborious process by women. The grains were placed on a large slab of stone and then ground by pushing a smaller stone back and forth. This process could consume two or more hours of a woman's life to produce enough flour for a family of six on a daily basis.

To bake the bread, women would use a communal oven that was dome-shaped and made of clay. These were probably used together by a few families. When Leviticus 26 speaks about the curses that will come upon Israel if they disobey God's command, it mentions that in the time of suffering ten women will bake bread in a single oven, but they will "eat and not be satisfied" (Lev 26:26). The verse indicates that ten sharing the same oven was a sign of difficult times and even the bread produced would not be sufficient.

Two other main food sources mentioned throughout the Old Testament are olive oil and wine. Olive trees can thrive in shallow, dry soil as their roots tap deep within the earth. Their fruit was a major source of dietary fat and was also useful for lamp oil when crushed. Likewise, grapes were pressed to make wine, which was the most common beverage among Israelites. It's estimated that adult men in the post-biblical world consumed a liter of wine per day.[5] Ancient Israelites may have drunk less, but wine was still the most important drink in their diet.

Other fruits that would have been eaten are those produced by indigenous trees like figs, dates, and pomegranates. Vegetables were almost entirely absent from the Israelite diet. These required significant amounts of water to grow. This led to nutritional deficiencies and increased susceptibility to disease.

The hardships of subsistence farming in ancient Israel should not be underestimated when reading the book of Leviticus. God's commands around eating and holiness were not just inconvenient dietary restrictions. They had real implications on what one could eat to survive. Food and faith are bound together in Leviticus as God taught his people to trust in him for their daily bread. Food also became a sign of holiness for Israel and a reminder that eating and purity were part of their covenant relationship. To be God's people meant committing every aspect of life to holiness.

Though environmental constraints often brought significant hardship to the average Israelite family, the Old Testament is also full of imagery that expresses God's overflowing and abundant blessings when his people are faithful. Like olive oil poured out, wine flowing, milk and honey, grain storehouses spilling over, Israel would enjoy the blessings of life in the land if they walked in holiness. But if they disobeyed, God would allow the cruel forces of nature that brought famine, blight, and disease to spread through their camp. This is why God implores the people to eat and live in holiness so that they might have peace in the land and experience his blessing. "And I will walk among you, and will be your God, and you shall be my people" (Lev 26:12).

HOLINESS AND EATING TODAY

Imagine some new neighbors have moved in next door. They come from a foreign country and seem very friendly. Over the summer they invite you round for a barbecue. They promise to offer you a great banquet of dishes from their home country to give you an authentic taste of the delicacies from their land. You've never eaten this type of cuisine before so you go with great anticipation and curiosity.

The couple warmly invite you into their home and outside on the patio you can see the smoke rising from the grill. The outdoor table is covered with an array of colorful dishes of vegetables, beans, and rice. The thick

---

5. Meyers, *Rediscovering Eve*, 48–49.

aroma of spices mixed with the scent of grilled meat makes your stomach growl in hunger as you can't wait to sit down and eat.

When everything is prepared you gather around the table and your host begins to point out all the different dishes and meats they've prepared. She points to one platter and explains that grilled camel, rock badger, and ostrich are delicacies in their country. Then she points to some lobster and crab alongside a plate of fried gecko and tells you that these are some of their favorites. Just before you eat your host interrupts to let you know that they have local gods in their country that they pray to and that it's a family tradition to offer food to them. They laugh and say that it's just an old superstition, but they still pray over their food as an offering to the gods.

Now, if you're a Jew following kosher laws for eating you're going to find yourself in a very difficult position and will probably stick to vegetables to be on the safe side lest you make yourself unclean by the other foods. But what if you're a Christian? What can you eat and is there anything you should not eat?

Food was a significant issue in the early church because Jews and gentiles were gathering together to worship and to eat as a sign of the new covenant community in Christ. It would have been difficult for a practicing Jew to give up the religious diet they had lived on their whole lives, but it was equally difficult to enforce the same restrictions on a gentile, especially if they were accustomed to eating pork three times a week!

The other challenge that these Christian communities faced was the fact that in the ancient world there was no separate category of life called "religion." If you asked an ancient Greek or Roman what "religion" they practiced, they might stare at you with a confused look on their face. The better question would be to ask what gods they worshipped, because the whole world was shaped and governed by the gods. This meant that all aspects of life, whether social, political, or economic, were under the guidance of the gods. This also applied to food. Nearly all the meat found in a normal marketplace in the ancient world had been sacrificed or dedicated to the gods. It would be like going to the meat section in a grocery store today and finding labels under the chickens or steaks that said, "Sacrificed to Brahma on 10/09/21."

Food and religion were deeply bound together in the ancient world, which made matters all the more complicated for both Jew and gentile followers of Jesus Christ. Should they obey the commands of Leviticus 11 as Jews had done for centuries? Should they abandon food restrictions? Jesus himself (even though he likely followed the dietary commands of Leviticus during his life) said that nothing going into a person makes them unclean, thus declaring all foods clean (Mark 7:18-20). How then should Christians, living under the new covenant, respond to issues around food and faith?

Many of the early followers of Jesus struggled with Jewish dietary regulations, primarily because of the mission to the gentiles. The first major discussion on the issue happened in Jerusalem when some Jews were enforcing Jewish practices (like circumcision) on gentile believers. The apostles who were gathered in Jerusalem debated the matter and came to their decision after hearing of the signs and wonders Paul and Barnabas experienced among the gentiles.

The apostle James declared that all gentiles should abstain from, "things polluted by idols and from fornication and from whatever has been strangled and from blood" (Acts 15:20). The first two prohibitions deal with worshipping false gods and sexual impurity, but the second two have to do with food. The apostles are reading back to the earliest ban on consuming blood given to Noah after the flood (Gen 9:4-6) and to the requirements of Leviticus. Their decision seems to rest on the Jewish association of blood with life and atonement which had been further revealed through the blood of Christ. Even in the new age of the Holy Spirit, blood was still the sole property of God and was not to be consumed in animal meat.

The apostle Paul took these instructions and expanded on them for the churches in Corinth who were struggling with decisions regarding food sacrificed to idols in the marketplace. Paul offers a detailed argument and begins, "Now concerning food sacrificed to idols: we know that 'all of us possess knowledge.' Knowledge puffs up, but love builds up" (1 Cor 8:1). This is to say that everyone *knows* there is a new freedom for believers in Christ through the indwelling Holy Spirit. Knowledge about what one can do with this new freedom, however, can "puff up" if it is not grounded in love that "builds up." A person may *know* what they can do as a follower of Christ, but that should always be guided by the *love* one demonstrates toward their neighbor.

Paul goes on for two more chapters to explain this principal of faith by stressing that though he is free in Christ, he makes himself a servant to others in love to bring them to Christ (1 Cor 8:19). As he comes to his conclusion he writes, "'All things are lawful,' but not all things are beneficial. 'All things are lawful,' but not all things build up" (1 Cor 10:23). His point is that though we have freedom in Christ, we use that freedom to serve and build up others in love so that ultimately we become imitators of Christ (1 Cor 11:1). So how does this all relate to food? Paul goes on and writes:

> Eat whatever is sold in the meat market without raising any question on the ground of conscience, for "the earth and its fullness

are the Lord's." If an unbeliever invites you to a meal and you are disposed to go, eat whatever is set before you without raising any question on the ground of conscience. But if someone says to you, "This has been offered in sacrifice," then do not eat it, out of consideration for the one who informed you, and for the sake of conscience—I mean the other's conscience, not your own. For why should my liberty be subject to the judgment of someone else's conscience? If I partake with thankfulness, why should I be denounced because of that for which I give thanks? So, whether you eat or drink, or whatever you do, do everything for the glory of God. (1 Cor 10:25-31)

All things come from God and all things have been sanctified through Christ. Paul says don't worry about other "gods" because they don't exist. You can eat whatever you want in Christ, but only when you do it in such a way that glorifies God. This doesn't mean that we can consume whatever we like, whenever we like, and as much as we like. What it does mean is that followers of Christ have the freedom to eat anything, but they do so in a way that always brings glory to God.

Let's go back to our situation at the beginning to see if we can answer our dilemma through Paul's wisdom. Should we eat a bit of camel or rock badger? Yes, we can (but you may not want to!). What if it was offered to the gods? Our knowledge tells us there are no other "gods" so we can still eat, but how might we handle the situation in love that "builds up"? There is no one right answer, and Paul was not giving one answer for every situation. The question to ask is, how could this scenario glorify God? Maybe your neighbor's comments might lead to a discussion on faith and thankfulness to God. It may be an opportunity to share the gospel of Christ and how that relates to your own eating and drinking. There are endless possibilities as to how the conversation might go, but Paul's point is to make sure that the goal is to demonstrate love for the glory of God.

If this is the principle that Christian's should follow in how they eat and drink, we might question whether our patterns of consumption in the modern world are leading toward the glory of God. We discussed above how the economic forces of the industrialized world have shaped our view of creation as a resource to be used, or exploited, to satisfy human appetites. We treat technology as tools to master our environment and food production rather than as a means to participate in the order and goodness of God's creation.

Industrialism and agribusinesses in the West have been driven by cheap production for the sake of increased profit. Wendell Berry laments that modern Christianity has, "stood silently by, while a predatory economy has ravaged the world, destroyed its natural beauty and health, divided and plundered its human communities and households."[6] This commodification of God's world stands in stark antithesis to the vision of Leviticus or that of the early Christian church, which viewed all life as a sacred gift to be treated with wisdom and love.

The holiness that emerges from the dietary rules in Leviticus is a holiness that recognizes our role within creation, to care and to keep it, in order that God's blessing and fertility might be made known. Israel must play its part by restricting what it consumes as a sign of faithfulness and commitment to God's commands and the purity of the tabernacle. When the people demonstrate this kind of faith and holiness, the psalmist praises God for the blessings he pours out in return. "You cause the grass to grow for the cattle, and plants for people to use, to bring forth food from the earth, and wine to gladden the human heart, oil to make the face shine, and bread to strengthen the human heart" (Ps 104:14–15). This celebration of God's provision is a song that should be sung by Christians today. Whether in our eating or drinking, we remember that the call to holiness is to sustain, to bless, to bring forth life, and to cause all creation to flourish as God intended.

Another ethical issue to consider when thinking about food and faith today is the practice of genetic modification. Ellen Davis highlights the fact that traditional mixing between similar species (plant or animal) has been a part of agrarian practice for centuries. However, modern engineering has given us the ability to split DNA, which has been used to mix plant, animal, and bacterial DNA.[7] The question we might ask is whether such combinations go against natural genetic compositions that preserve the integrity of individual organisms. Davis argues that regard for the natural divisions within the created order in Leviticus demonstrate a wisdom and respect for creation that "should guide us in determining what might constitute holiness with respect to our culture's scientific, agricultural, and eating practices."[8] These issues, along with others, continue to raise questions over modern food production and whether or not it adheres to the principles of honoring and caring for God's creation and what we consume.

The dietary requirements of Leviticus may seem like relics from an ancient past that have nothing to do with Christian faith today. We've seen, however, that undergirding these rules is a fundamental respect for the sanctity and integrity of all creation. Leviticus teaches us that discipleship must be wholistic where everything we do, whether we eat or drink, should

---

6. Berry, "Christianity and the Survival of Creation," 162.
7. Davis, *Scripture, Culture, and Agriculture*, 87–88.
8. Davis, *Scripture, Culture, and Agriculture*, 90.

be done to the glory of God. Though dietary regulations change in the New Testament, the principles of eating and drinking remain the same. The early Christians struggled with how to live in their new freedom in Christ through the food they ate, but Paul reminds them to go back to the foundations of love and holiness. How we eat, how we care for the land, and how we treat the animals of God's creation all relate to our growth into God's image and our unity in the body of Christ. Wendell Berry sums this up when he writes, "The Bible leaves no doubt at all about the sanctity of the act of world-making, or of the world that was made, or of creaturely or bodily life in this world. We are holy creatures living among other holy creatures in a world that is holy."[9]

---

9. Berry, "Christianity and the Survival of Creation," 152.

5

Living in Holy Time

Finding God's Rhythm

A SEASON FOR ALL THINGS

One way to learn about a culture is to participate in the rhythm of its festival year. Celebrations, feasts, or rites of passage all convey something about peoples' understanding of God, humanity, and life. This is particularly true of the Christian festival calendar which finds its earliest roots in Leviticus and God's commands concerning the division and celebration of time.

The writer of Ecclesiastes expresses what is central to the annual life of a holy people. "For everything there is a season, and a time for every matter under heaven" (Eccl 3:1). To understand holiness in Leviticus we must also grasp what it means to live in *holy time* and to celebrate "sacred occasions" or "holy convocations" throughout the year. These fixed times in Israel's calendar brought them together as a community in their celebrations and turned their eyes toward God as they remembered his mighty works of salvation and his ongoing provision.

For a largely illiterate population, annual festivals become a means of teaching and reminding people of their roots. The Israelites were always in danger of forgetting their calling to be a holy people, but annual celebrations acted as constant reminders of who God is and who they are as his chosen ones. These breaks from everyday life allowed the people to suspend their normal activities and enter into holy time together.

Sacred occasions were not just moments to remember the past. The festivals that God prescribes are to *re-actualize* historic events so that they have an ever-present meaning. In this way, God's past works of salvation become present realities that help shape the faith and belief of his people. Festivals helped Israel look back to God's power to save and to reflect on God's future liberation and blessing.

Take, for example, the Passover festival and its rituals. We find a sacred occasion that looks back to God's deliverance from Egypt, considers his power to act in the present, and looks forward to his coming salvation. This would have been a vital reminder for those Jews who celebrated the Passover in exile and for those during Jesus' day who were under the foreign rule of the Roman Empire.

Festival calendars were common throughout the ancient world. Most civilizations ordered their years around the lunar calendar and sacred days were often connected with times of harvest. The most significant points in the year were the vernal and autumnal equinoxes. For ancient Israel the spring equinox was linked to the barley and wheat harvests. The autumnal equinox came at the end of harvest and at the beginning of preparations for the winter rains.

There are two places in the Old Testament that provide a list of all the festivals that Israel is to celebrate. The first is in Leviticus 23 and a similar, but slightly different, version can be found in Numbers 28–29. The calendar in Numbers highlights the prescribed sacrifices while Leviticus focuses on holiness and emphasizes the Sabbath rhythm of work and rest. Festivals were like public holidays that gave people a break from their normal work schedules to be with family and friends. They also offered a great excuse to bring the whole community together for a party with plenty of eating and drinking.

In the early days of Israel's life in the land these festivals would have been celebrated by local communities. Over time, many of these holy days were moved to the central sanctuary in Jerusalem. Some festivals became associated with pilgrimage for Jews who lived far away from the temple. We see this during Jesus' day as he and his disciples often joined the throngs in Jerusalem for festivals like Passover and Pentecost. Whether in local communities or at the temple in Jerusalem, festivals were another way for God to teach his people about their relationship with him and the blessing he offers to his people through sacred time and celebration.

HOLY TIME VERSUS CONSUMER TIME

The practice of celebrating sacred occasions throughout the year drew the covenant community together, released them from their daily work, and gave them the space to recall God's goodness and presence in the world. God had established the movements of the sun, moon, and stars from the beginning of creation to offer an order for liturgical time. Even after the flood God promises Noah that, "As long as the earth endures, seedtime and harvest, cold and heat, summer and winter, day and night, shall not cease" (Gen 8:22). Consistent cycles throughout the year offered stability and some level of predictability in an unpredictable world. It also meant that Israel could look to the rhythms of the heavenly bodies established by God to divide the calendar into different times and seasons. There were no clocks, watches, or digital calendars sending incessant notifications. Life was governed by the celestial bodies, all created and sustained by the hand of God.

Without the consistent rhythm of our solar system it's hard to imagine what life would be like. What if the sun didn't rise consistently each day? What if the earth's rotation around the sun was erratic and inconsistent so that there was no regularity between day and night? What if the moon didn't orbit the earth once every 27.322 days and we couldn't calculate months or years? Though modern science tells us that these things must happen according to the laws of physics, imagine how unsettled life would be if these patterns were disrupted and we couldn't rely on them to have some sense of calculating time.

It's within order that we find freedom. In Leviticus it's God who provides this order and establishes consistent rhythms in creation so that his people can experience holy times and sacred occasions. Life without these types of interruptions blurs into monotony. Work becomes dull and spiritless as we repeat the same things over and over. As human beings we are in need of both constancy and change. Celebrations of holy time throughout our yearly calendars act like sacred intrusions that disrupt the monotones of work with the piercing jolt of heavenly choirs. Like angels announcing the birth of a Savior, we awaken to a world where God is in our midst.

It is from the cosmological order that Israel finds its liturgical order. The division of time is based on the divisions of creation that culminate in the seventh day of Sabbath rest. This same pattern is found in the building of the tabernacle when Moses, like God, "finishes his work" (Exod 40:33). After the tent structure is complete, God's glory descends.

In Leviticus the next stage comes on the "eighth day" (Lev 9:1) when God comes down to consecrate the altar. This dramatic moment marks the beginning of Israel's festival calendar when sacrifices can begin to take place.

From this time forward Israel will set aside specific days to remember God's presence with them, the works he has done to save them, and his continued provision and blessing upon them.

It's difficult to think about holy time in a secular world where sayings like, "Time is money" dominate the spirit of our culture. Even time can become a commodity in a consumer world. Our work lives can become a means to an end with wealth as the primary goal. There is no space for holy time within a consumer society. Instead, we find corporations creating their own liturgy of summer sales, Black Friday, end of season clearances, or even transforming Christian holy days into consumer feasts. When we think about Christmas and Easter we might be more inclined these days to think about presents or chocolate eggs rather than the birth or resurrection of Christ.

The liturgy of the consumer world is defined by its great cathedrals—shopping malls. In his book, *You Are What You Love*, James K. A. Smith offers an insightful description of these open-planned consumer worship spaces. They are filled with glass and light and towering ceilings that give the shopper a sense of vertical wonder like some medieval cathedral. We raise our eyes toward the heavens not to see God, however, but to gaze upon the multitude of glimmering signs that identify the branded storefronts.

Smith describes how when we enter the mall we are protected from the clamor of the outside world and are invited to leave our worries behind as we're lured in to make our purchases. The consumer is familiar with the signs and symbols of the mall. They find peace in brand recognition, knowing that wherever they go in the world, the quality of their favorite stores will always be a welcome and familiar sight.[1]

Smith goes on to describe the sense of timelessness one experiences inside the mall as shoppers are released from their mundane lives to indulge in a bit of consumption. There is no liturgy of time, but "it almost seems as if the sun stands still in this space as we lose consciousness of time's passing and so lose ourselves in the rituals for which we've come."[2] The only thing that defines change in the seasonal calendar of the mall is the cycle of decorations that mark the beginnings of new movements in the shopping year.

Worship in the mall takes on a different form. As Smith writes:

> When invited to worship here, we are not only invited to give; we are invited to take. We don't leave this transformative experience with just good feeling or pious generalities, but rather with something concrete and tangible—with newly minted relics, as

---

1. Smith, *You Are What You Love*, 40–46.
2. Smith, *You Are What You Love*, 42.

it were, which are themselves the means to the good life embodied in the icons who invited us into this participatory moment in the first place.[3]

The worship of the consumer world is not one of gratitude or of offering gifts back to God. It's our opportunity to turn our attention from the world to our own satisfaction, to walk away with more disposable things, and to feel a fleeting moment of fulfillment.

The rhythm of the consumer world is one that stands in opposition to holy time. God's appointed seasons, defined by the movement of heavenly bodies, were to draw his people together as a community of faith and to call them back to their identity as his beloved. Holy days were reminders of what God had done to bring about his salvation and signs that pointed to hope in his future blessings. Holy time binds the community of faith together and reminds them of their role in the world to be a reflection of God's holiness.

Consumer time, however, has nothing to do with God's time. It's not concerned with the cosmos or the external world. It defines its own times and seasons through artificial lights and ever-changing ornamentation and trimmings. Consumer time is self-centered. Though we may go shopping with others, there is little if any emphasis on drawing together the wider community. The primary focus of consumerism is personal transaction and self-satisfaction. When we buy something we satisfy our own desires regardless of how it effects our neighbor. Oftentimes our purchasing may even be to the detriment of others or to the environment. Consumer time is about the individual and self-satisfaction whereas holy time turns us outward to encounter the love of God and neighbor.

The liturgy of the consumer world is also identity-forming, but the message is not that you are beloved by God. The message is that you need to purchase more to be happy, to be pretty, to be loved, and to enjoy the good life that you deserve. Redemption is experienced only in the brief moment of buying that item you always wanted. The feeling quickly fades, however, before you need to go back for more. In this cycle there is no future hope beyond the satisfaction of purchasing the latest product or having the newest gadget. Unlike holy times and seasons that celebrate and re-actualize moments in the history of salvation with a hope for future redemption, consumer time leads down a dark and endless spiral of consumption and disposal that leaves us perpetually unsatisfied.

Whether we like it or not, the liturgies of the consumer world have influenced our understanding of times and seasons. We have bought into its narrative of desire, need, and disposal and oftentimes have attached these to

---

3. Smith, *You Are What You Love*, 45.

traditional holy days of the church. Our self-worth and identity have been swayed by the message that we're not worthy, we're not beautiful, and that we'll never be happy unless we have the latest products. But Leviticus invites us into a different world. It's the sacred world of God's order and beauty where holy patterns are established according to his time. Leviticus offers a liturgy that brings rest, restoration, and the formation of God's people into a holy nation that reflects his light to the world.

A SACRED CALENDAR

Leviticus 23 sets out the order for the calendar year. The liturgy of God's people is one that is rooted in harvest and the story of salvation. The seasons call to mind the most significant events of redemption in the exodus from Egypt and God's continued provision of their daily bread.

The year is divided into two halves. The first half begins in the spring with the festivals of Passover and Unleavened Bread (Lev 23:4–8), First Fruits (vv. 9–14), and the Feast of Weeks (Pentecost) (vv. 15–22). The second half of the year is marked by autumnal celebrations in the seventh month with the festival of Trumpets (vv. 15–22), the Day of Atonement (vv. 26–32), and the festival of Booths (vv. 33–36, 39–43). In both halves we find that key moments of the exodus are remembered alongside the patterns of harvest and seeding.

The cornerstone of the calendar in Leviticus is the Sabbath. The pattern of working for six days followed by a seventh day of complete rest is critical in ordering the year. The number seven in the Old Testament represents wholeness and so we see that there are seven annual festivals, which are often marked by seven days of rest. Every seventh year was a sabbatical year for the land and after the forty-ninth year (7 x 7) was the celebration of Jubilee.[4]

The practice of Sabbath rest and ceasing from all work on the seventh day is a sign of trust and obedience. The pattern follows God's creative ways in the universe and the fourth commandment reminds Israel that they are to rest because, "in six days the LORD made heaven and earth, the sea, and all that is in them, but rested the seventh day; therefore the LORD blessed the sabbath day and consecrated it" (Exod 20:11). Leviticus emphasizes the necessity for a "sabbath of complete rest" or an "absolute sabbath" (Lev 23:3) for all of Israel on the seventh day. This likely took place from evening to evening, which is the common practice among Jews today.

---

4. For more on the Sabbath and its importance for Christians today, see my *Sabbath Rest: The Beauty of God's Rhythm for a Digital Age*.

God consecrated the seventh day in the very beginning of creation. He set time apart as holy so that he might rest. We might be slightly surprised that the biblical authors would be willing to depict God as needing rest after a long week of work. God didn't need to rest, but he sets an example for his children so that they might learn what it means to follow his rhythm. In Egypt the Israelites were slaves that worked without ceasing until their lives often came to a premature end. As the liberated people of God, however, they are commanded to practice his rest and to bring refreshment to their families, their servants, the foreigners among them, their farm animals, and even their land.

Though God consecrated the seventh day at the beginning of creation, Israel is commanded to reconsecrate, or set aside, the Sabbath as holy each week. They too are to cease from their work and relinquish any profit or gain they might have made. They are to find rest and refreshment by relaxing together with family and friends. Sabbath in the Old Testament is not merely about one's personal rest (though it does accomplish this) but, rather, it emphasizes the power of communal rest when we cease from work together. Sabbath is about bringing families and communities together one day a week without the pressing demands of work. For Jesus and his disciples this meant gathering in the synagogue to study God's word and then eating together in the home. This may have offered the disciples some of the few quiet moments they had with Jesus throughout his ministry.

The holiness of the Sabbath in Leviticus also seems to be placed on equal status with the holiness of the sanctuary. Prior to Leviticus 23 we read God's command, "You shall keep my sabbaths and reverence my sanctuary: I am the LORD" (Lev 19:30; 26:2). To keep the Sabbath requires the same state of reverence one might have when approaching God's tabernacle. The idea here is that *the holiness of time is equivalent to the holiness of place*. We encounter God when we consecrate holy time by keeping the Sabbath and this is no less awesome than approaching his presence in the tabernacle.

Work, rest, and celebration are all necessary for human beings to thrive and to grow into the holiness that God desires. Though many Christians associate Leviticus with endless laws on sacrifice and purity, there is a deeper layer that we discover in the Sabbath command. God is concerned with our growth individually and collectively toward wholeness through the rhythm of Sabbath and the consecration of time. Sabbath is not only one day of rest each week. It's a movement toward wholeness and the consecration of all things.

We capture this vision in Revelation 21 when there will be no more need of a temple because, "the home of God is among mortals. He will dwell with them as their God; they will be his peoples, and God himself will be with them" (Rev 21:3). In the end there will be no need for Sabbath or even the sun or moon because the glory of God will be the light and peace of all nations (Rev 21:22–24).

The Sabbath is an anticipation of the joy that will come when God is fully united to his children once more. In this earthly life, however, holy time is critical in the journey of a pilgrim people who are in need of being refreshed. Jewish scholar Abraham Heschel reflects on the history of the Sabbath in Jewish practice.

> Judaism is a *religion of time* aiming at the *sanctification of time* . . . Judaism teaches us to be attached to the *holiness in time*, to be attached to sacred events, to learn how to consecrate sanctuaries that emerge from the magnificent stream of the year. The Sabbaths are our great cathedrals.[5]

For Jews and Christians, to experience "holiness in time" is to begin to taste the eternality of God's presence in this world and to witness the coming of his kingdom on earth as it is in heaven.

The sanctification of time and keeping the Sabbath was to help Israel find anchor points in the endless stream of seasons and years. To gather together, to worship, to eat and rest, all without the burden of work, is a way in which families and the community of faith can grow in holiness. In Leviticus the calendar year emerges from the pattern of the seventh day of holy ceasing, consecrating, and entering into the promise of God's rest.

Sabbath practice was alive and well during Jesus' day. Even after Pentecost, the apostles continued to worship at the temple or in synagogues on the Sabbath as they proclaimed the good news of Christ as Messiah. Like most conflicts in the early church, there was some question about whether gentiles should maintain the Sabbath. Though the history of Sabbath practice varies in the early church, the majority of Christians began to gather on "the Lord's day," or Sunday, the day of resurrection (cf. Rev 1:10). This ultimately became the day of worship for Christians while others continued to keep the Sabbath on Saturdays.

Later Christian tradition adapted the patterns of the Jewish liturgical year but celebrated the events of the life, death, resurrection, and ascension of Christ. Like Jewish festivals based on the lunar calendar, some Western Christian holy days (like Easter) followed the same pattern. Christmas, however, was fixed on December 25th in the fourth century AD, which took the place of Roman pagan festivals around the winter solstice.

---

5. Heschel, *Sabbath*, 8.

The establishment of yearly liturgies in the church continued to develop through the monastic tradition. The specific cycle of daily prayer became known as the divine office. This was thought to parallel the heavenly pattern of marking out seven specific times for prayer following the psalmist who writes, "seven times a day I have praised you" (Ps 119:164). Monks would pray at Lauds (5am), Prime (6am), Terce (9am), Sext (noon), None (3pm), Vespers (6pm), and Compline (7pm). They would also rise for Vigils around 3:30am again following the psalmist, who declares, "at midnight I arose to give you praise" (Ps 118:62). St. Benedict established this pattern in his monasteries through a simple rule to help the brothers order their lives around the heavenly pattern of worship and prayer.

A form of the daily office that includes holy days throughout the year is practiced in many Christian traditions today, but others have jettisoned the structure altogether. Some think it's too formal, too rigid, or too ritualistic, but it remains a form of holy time and liturgy that has existed in the church for centuries. And, as we have seen, it was a practice that God instituted among his people for the sake of their growth in holiness.

The liturgical calendar that God established for his people didn't offer tortuous notifications like our digital devices do today. The marking of specific times and seasons did, however, bring them back to the story of salvation and their identity as a covenant people. The Christian calendar offers the same purpose with the intent of drawing together the body of Christ in celebration of what God has done and what he will do in the future.

THE JEWISH FESTIVALS

Passover and Unleavened Bread

The yearly celebration of Passover and Unleavened Bread focused on the climactic events of the exodus. God's decisive victory over Pharaoh and Egypt was commemorated by remembering the blood of protection placed on the doorposts and the bread without leaven made in haste before their departure. Egypt was struck with the death of their firstborn while Israel was preserved and finally set free.

The annual celebration of the Passover events became an ever-present reality for each generation of Israelites who identified themselves with their ancestors as they anticipated God's deliverance from their enemies. Though different Passover rituals may have taken shape over generations (cf. Ezek 45:21–25), there was only one Passover feast at the beginning of each liturgical year as a sign of re-birth and new life.

The Passover marked a time of new beginnings. When Moses first announced the festival to the people he said, "This month shall mark for you the beginning of months; it shall be the first month of the year for you" (Exod 12:1). It was celebrated on the fourteenth of Nisan which was the first month after the spring equinox. In some ways, Passover was like a birthday celebration for the Israelites. In their release from Egypt God would give them new life as his covenant people. Prior to this, in Genesis, God's covenant was with Abraham, Isaac, and Jacob, but now an entire people group would enter into relationship with him. This national identification was a powerful reminder of their former years of slavery and the sovereignty of God over the nations to deliver them from death to life.

Though the Passover commemorates the birth of Israel, it was also to be observed by the "alien who resides among you" (Exod 12:49; Num 9:14). We remember that a "mixed multitude" went out of Egypt with Israel (Exod 12:38), which means that many other slaves from different countries also experienced salvation when they departed with the Israelites. In the wilderness wanderings, God commands Israel regarding the foreigners or sojourners among them. They are given protected status under the law and are not to be mistreated (Exod 12:48; 22:1; 23:9; Lev 19:33–34; 24:22). In Leviticus, this concern for justice among all those dwelling within the covenant community offers a vision for how both Jew and foreigner could consecrate holy festivals together. If God included non-Hebrew slaves in his movement of salvation from Egypt, then the community of Israel should commemorate the occasion equally with those foreigners who dwell in their households.

The First Fruits

The second festival of the year is the first fruits, which is tied to Israel's life in the land. The people are to bring an offering of the first fruits of the harvest in gratitude for what God had provided. The priests are to wave the grain offering before the altar after the Sabbath that follows the final day of the feast of Unleavened Bread (Lev 23:11). Along with the first sheaths of barley, the people must also offer a year-old lamb without blemish and a grain offering mixed with oil and a drink offering of wine.

The first fruits was an agricultural festival that reminded the people of the abundant bounty that the Lord provided from the land. Its celebration was not only about provision of food, but it was also a political and religious declaration that their God—rather than Baal, the Canaanite god of fertility—is the Lord of the harvest. We remember that these festivals were celebrated among Israel's Canaanite neighbors, who had their own gods and celebrations. To bring the first fruits to God was a symbolic act that defied the religion and beliefs of those native to the land.

Despite God's commands, we find that Baal worship plays a significant role in the history of God's people. Even during the period before the destruction of Jerusalem Jeremiah laments, "For your gods have become as many as your towns, O Judah; and as many as the streets of Jerusalem are the altars you have set up to shame, altars to make offerings to Baal" (Jer 11:13). Despite king Josiah's efforts only a few decades earlier to destroy all the altars in the land (2 Kgs 23:19), it appears that the people continued to celebrate the appointed festivals in Jerusalem while also making offerings at their local shrines to other gods.

The festival of first fruits was likely rooted in Israel's ancient agricultural practices of offering gifts to God from the first harvest of the year. This was later transformed into part of Israel's liturgical calendar that became connected to the exodus events. The produce is not just an offering of thanksgiving, but it looks forward to God's provision of land promised to the patriarchs and fulfilled through Moses and Joshua.

Offering the first fruits was also a yearly reminder of Israel's dependency on the Lord of the land (Lev 25:23). All of the harvest belongs to God, but he graciously gives it to his children. We find a similar sentiment in the prohibitions around fruit trees when Israel enters into the land. They must not touch the trees for the first three years and the fruit of the fourth year must be wholly offered to God. Only in the fifth year can they partake of the fruit of the land (Lev 19:23–25). This is another sign of trust and thanksgiving for the produce that comes from the Lord.

The Feast of Weeks (*Shavuot*)

The third and final festival of the spring once again celebrates the harvest. The Israelites are to count off seven Sabbaths (forty-nine days) following the offering of the first fruits. On the fiftieth day (or "Pentecost" from the Greek) after the final Sabbath they are to bring another offering to the Lord. The period of fifty days marks the end of the barley harvest and the beginning of the wheat harvest. It's not exactly clear why there was a need to wait fifty days between the crops. It's possible that counting for seven weeks may have been a reminder to pray during a time when crops may have been susceptible to natural forces that might have destroyed that years' produce.

The period of seven Sabbath weeks is also a foreshadowing of the seven Sabbath years of rest for the land that culminate on the fiftieth year of Jubilee. The annual celebration of the Feast of Weeks prompted Israel to give thanks and to remember their calling to care for the land and for the welfare of the people dwelling in the land, especially the poor and those in need. Pentecost provided a yearly reminder of God's desire for justice and liberation in the land as it looked forward to the Jubilee when release and restoration would come (Isa 61:1–4).

In later Jewish tradition Pentecost was associated with Moses' receiving God's commandments at Mt. Sinai. In the Christian tradition, Pentecost marks the birth of the church with the outpouring of the Holy Spirit upon all peoples (Acts 2). The remarkable event was the catalyst for the gospel going out to the nations, which began with the abundance of pilgrims from foreign lands who had come to Jerusalem. The gift of the Spirit also resonated with the festival's original themes. The Lord of the harvest pours out the abundance of his goodness upon his people as they are reminded of those in need or those who suffer in poverty on the margins of society. One of the first signs of the early church in Jerusalem was its generous giving to the poor and provision for the widows (Acts 2:42–47; 4:32–37; 6:1–2). As a foreshadowing of the Jubilee, Pentecost also celebrates release and restoration, which now comes through Christ's sacrifice and the release from sin and death.

The Feast of Weeks marked the end of the three major spring festivals that recalled God's redemption of his people from Egypt and his provision for them in the promised land. The yearly cycle of the barley and wheat harvests offered a time to gather together to celebrate the God who saves and the God who provides. The Lord who brings freedom, salvation, joy, security, and life is also the God who pours out his Spirit in full measure upon the nations to draw all peoples into his church.

The Day of Trumpets

The Day of Trumpets, or the Day of "Blasts," marks the first day of the seventh month, which later came to be the Jewish new year. This is the first in a series of festivals in the seventh month that marks the end of the hot, dry summer season. It's a time to prepare for the new agricultural year as Israel awaited the winter rains. Work on the land was at a minimum, which allowed time for mental, physical, and spiritual refreshment as well as anticipation of the harvest for the coming year.

In ancient Israel the horn (*shofar*) was used to gather people together, to sound an alarm, or to prepare the troops for battle. The loud, piercing noise could be heard for great distances and was an important instrument for designating significant moments. It was traditionally made from a ram's horn with its spiral shape and is still used in synagogues today.

The loud noise was an audible reminder to arouse God's people to pray as they looked forward to a new year of harvest and hoped for enough rain. The reverberation of the *shofar* through the towns and cities of Israel was an audible interruption that shattered the monotony of the average workday. Sound and music create compelling reminders to inspire communities to wake from their routines and enliven memories and emotions associated with particular times or seasons.

There are many audible reminders that Christians associate with the liturgical calendar today. The sound of Christmas carols or Handel's *Messiah* draws us back to the birth of Christ and all that we associate with Advent and the Christmas season. Other hymns evoke memories of Easter or Pentecost. Music and sound are interconnected with our experience of the world. For ancient Israel, it was the power of the *shofar* pealing out from the heights to announce the beginning of a new year.

The Day of Atonement (*Yom Kippur*)

We have spoken about the specifics of the Day of Atonement in chapter 2, so here we'll discuss how it sits within the calendar year. Ten days after the trumpet's blast, the people of Israel were reminded of their individual and communal sins that had defiled God's holy sanctuary. This festival is defined by sacrifice, abstaining from work, and fasting. The whole nation was called to repentance, self-examination, and mourning for the sake of purifying themselves and the sanctuary that had been stained by their sin.

The command to cease from work was common for most festival days, but on *Yom Kippur* the weight of such a practice is brought into perspective. Anyone who does not fast will be "cut off" from the community (Lev 23:29), which is basically the equivalent of the death penalty. To be cut off from one's family and community was possibly the worst thing that could happen to anyone in the ancient world. The threat of punishment comes directly from the hand of the Lord. "And anyone who does any work during that entire day, such a one I will destroy from the midst of the people" (Lev 23:30). This is the only time in Leviticus where God threatens to inflict punishment on a person by his own hand. Such is the importance of setting aside one day a year as a whole community to repent of sins and be reminded of God's mercy in allowing for atonement to be made.

The purification of the people and the sanctuary on an annual basis was one of the most significant rituals performed throughout the year. The sacrifices, detailed in Leviticus 16, are reminders of the need for repentance, purity, and holiness. Whether through intentional or unintentional sins, the pollution of Israel's transgression must be remembered and atoned for to preserve the people and ensure the ongoing presence of God in the tabernacle.

Throughout the history of the church, the seasons of Advent and Lent have been traditionally associated with repentance and fasting. In the early Roman church there were also "Ember days" that required fasting for three days throughout the four seasons of the year. Following the practice of God's commands to Israel, Christians recognized the importance of repentance and meditation on God's forgiveness and mercy. Though the act of atonement in Christ was made once-for-all, days for fasting and repentance were incorporated throughout the Christian liturgical year as constant reminders of God's grace, the gift of Christ's sacrifice, and care for the poor. These days draw us back to our journey toward holiness and remind us of humanity's ongoing need for repentance.

The Festival of Booths (*Sukkot*)

The final festival of the year is one of joy. Five days after repenting of their sins and cleansing the sanctuary, the Israelites are called to "rejoice before the LORD your God for seven days" (Lev 23:40). This is the only festival in Leviticus where rejoicing is actually commanded. The joy comes from a ritual that looks back to the exodus once again and recalls the wanderings in the wilderness and God's provision.

The Festival of Booths became one of the major pilgrimage festivals of the year (cf. Deut 16:13) and it's the only festival in which Israel is commanded to build something as a memorial to recall their ancestors' journey through the wilderness. The "booths" (*sukkot*) are to be constructed on the first day of the festival and should be made from "the fruit of majestic trees, branches of palm trees, boughs of leafy trees, and willows of the brook" (Lev 23:40). The term "majestic trees" is only used here in the Pentateuch and the description inspires images of Eden and the fertile land that God had promised to Abraham and his descendants. This sign of fertility stands in stark opposition to the barren wilderness of the Sinai Peninsula and acts as a reminder of the promise of God's blessing.

The ritual act of building a booth provides an experience for families to create something with their own hands. The physicality of the ritual is critical to the message that it conveys. God invites his people to re-create sacred space each year to remember his salvation. They are to leave the shelter and comfort of their homes, lie beneath palm branches, and gaze up at the stars as a reminder of how God provided for their ancestors when they wandered through the wilderness after leaving Egypt.

The creation of sacred space, and dwelling in that space, during the festival requires a break from normal routines. If you can imagine living in a booth with your family for seven days, you'll quickly understand how this can turn daily life upside down! But in the process of this change, the ritual also raises questions. Why in the world are we doing this? What if it rains? Whose idea was this anyway? The questions then provide opportunities to reflect and teach about God and what he has done on behalf of his people.

The physical act of building and dwelling in a newly constructed space is a powerful tool to teach and pass down traditions. For Israel it provided the opportunity to recall their ancestors' wandering through the wilderness, God's provision of manna, quail, and water, and his guidance to the promised land. The wilderness also reminded the people of their disobedience and their striving with God and testing his faithfulness (cf. Psalm 95). In the Festival of Booths, families become actors in the divine drama as they remember the God of their ancestors and his faithfulness in the wilderness.

After the destruction of Jerusalem and the Babylonian exile, the Jewish celebration of *Sukkot* is recalled in Neh 8:14–18, where every family in Jerusalem constructs a booth on the roof of their house. The people spend seven days listening to Ezra read from the book of the law (Neh 8:18) and all the people rejoiced. This is one of the few windows into post-exilic Jerusalem, and it gives us a picture of a people trying to find their roots once again. Their city had been destroyed, family members killed, and they had been exiled to a foreign land. Their return home and their rootedness in the land takes shape in their practice of an ancient festival and ritual of constructing a booth. This simple gesture ties them to the exodus, the works of God in the past, and the hope of his salvation for a new generation.

During Jesus' day the Jews had developed other rituals around the Festival of Booths. One of them included processing around the altar at the Jerusalem temple while waving palm branches. During each day of the feast, the priests would collect a golden pitcher of water from the pools of Siloam, which was poured out to the west and east of the altar. The ritual act was a sign and prayer for God to bless the coming season with the water needed for the crops.

On the seventh, and climactic, day of this festival we're told that Jesus entered the temple, stood up among the crowd of pilgrims and cried out, "Let anyone who is thirsty come to me, and let the one who believes in me drink. As the scripture has said, 'Out of the believer's heart shall flow rivers of living water'" (John 7:37–38). The gospel author goes on to explain that

Jesus said this about the Spirit who was to come (7:39) as a sign of God's new movement of salvation. Jesus takes the liturgy and rhythm of Israel's life and unveils its deeper meaning through his life and sacrifice. The festival becomes a sign of the multiple layers of God's salvation for his people in the past, present, and the future when he will pour out his Spirit on all nations.

HOLY TIME AND TECHNOLOGY

One of the greatest challenges that stands in the way of contemporary Christians experiencing holy time is technology. We have noted that sacred occasions and festivals were prescribed by God as a means of sacred interruption in our lives that draw us back to him and into communion with one another. Technology, on the other hand, can twist our perception of time. Our internet use and reliance on digital devices has the potential to lead to isolation, distraction, and addiction.

The effects of social media, especially on young people, continue to be researched, but many of the findings paint a bleak picture of social isolation, anxiety, and stress. Sherry Turkle's compelling book, *Alone Together*, documents some of the changes experienced by a generation of young people who are always connected through social media and yet feel an immense sense of loneliness. Throughout the book she explores how digital technologies and social media are affecting our social lives and our ability to engage with others face-to-face. She describes our predicament with clarity when she writes, "We fill our days with ongoing connection, denying ourselves time to think and dream. Busy to the point of depletion, we make a new Faustian bargain. It goes something like this: if we are left alone when we make contact, we can handle being together."[6]

One result of such developments in human behavior is our inability to set aside and allow for moments of sacred time. If we are consumed with managing our social-media feeds, online shopping, chat groups, or endless research, it can lead to exhaustion and isolation. We then lose the capacity to distinguish between times and seasons because we become lost in an online world where hours, days, weeks, and months blur together into a formless void. Our experience of time becomes distorted as we gaze into our screens for hours on end in a seemingly timeless online world.

The result is that there is little, if any, room for holy moments or sacred time. Our days can quickly become ordered according to how often we pick up our phones or stare at our computers rather than by daily cycles of prayer. Festival days might be celebrated in the presence of others but are

---

6. Turkle, *Alone Together*, 203.

often interrupted by endless selfies and posts to make sure that the event is documented online to keep up with our virtual connections. Holy times and seasons invite us to reflect on God's great works of salvation, his provision, and who we are as his covenant people, but digital technologies have the capacity to undermine these sacred moments. Rather than the experience of refreshment, fellowship, and joy, technology can lead us to a place of loneliness with the endless burden of always trying to keep up.

Another challenge we face with technology today is the ongoing distraction and disruption it creates in our daily lives. The digital world is non-stop and waits for no one. Viral sensations that spread across the globe are newsworthy one minute but forgotten the next. All the while we receive countless notifications that interrupt our days and reduce our ability to concentrate for any significant length of time. With so many distractions in our lives we are left with little space for holy intrusions and sacred occasions.

In Leviticus we saw that a rhythm of life was established around the seasonal patterns in the year and the movement of the heavenly bodies. Weekly work was interrupted by the Sabbath as a distinct holy day of rest. Spring and autumnal months were interspersed with festivals of harvest and recalling God's works of salvation. What is taken for granted in this rhythm of living is that there are moments of "ordinary time" where work and life move on in the normal way. The difficulty, however, for the contemporary urban dweller is that we can struggle to find any kind of ordinary time in daily life. The internet and our digital devices have so permeated our lives that they create a world besieged by interruption to the point where life becomes merely a series of interruptions.

We no longer give ourselves the space to reflect or to think long and deep on subjects without being distracted. Continued studies in neuroscience have demonstrated how our levels of engagement with internet technologies are affecting the hard wiring of our brains. In some instances, this has left us with low concentration levels or the inability to perform certain tasks because of cognitive decline due to atrophy in parts of the brain. A quick glance at the Pew Research Center's (www.pewresearch.com) work on the effects of internet technologies offers eye-opening testimonies to some of their negative impacts. From your average person to experts in the field of neuroscience, many bear witness to the detriments the internet is having on our ability to think. Though there are some positive statements about the contribution technology has made to society, the negative assessments should alert us to the fact that not everything we do with the internet leads to our growth as human beings.[7]

---

7. See Carr, *The Shallows* and *The Glass Cage*.

The problem is that the more we adjust and live with constant distraction in our lives, the more we get accustomed to it and the less potential we have to attune ourselves to sacred time. Let me offer an example. I was attending a piano recital by one of the world's leading pianists. It took place in an old concert hall that was shaped like a small amphitheater with long, curved wooden pews. As the pianist began what was a rather long and enchanting piece, I began to notice that every once in a while someone would shift in their seat which would produce an awful creaking noise. At one point, during a dramatic crescendo that was followed by a pregnant moment of silence, someone shifted and a loud creak completely ruined the moment!

Now imagine if the kingdom of God is like that piano piece. The rhythm of the music is like the rhythm of the liturgical year. It rises in moments to bold heights, and then softly guides us back down through subtle and gentle tones. At some points the tempo picks up rapidly stirring our excitement and then slows to bring us back to a moment of rest. Each movement and tone awakens our emotions and draws us into the story that the piece is trying to tell. However, it's very difficult to listen to that story if we're constantly being distracted by creaking pews.

When we are consumed by unceasing digital interruptions in our lives, it's like trying to attune ourselves to the piano piece while everyone is rocking back and forth in their seats, munching on nuts and slurping their drinks. The incessant noise prevents us from entering into the gift of the music. Soon we become so accustomed to the erratic disturbances that we no longer hear the music at all. This is the danger of losing our sense of sacred time in the modern world.

The liturgy of the year was God's way of drawing Israel back to the story of salvation and back to one another. The distractions of work were set aside, as they were each Sabbath, to gather together in thanksgiving for God's mercy and grace. But this pattern is easily undermined when we allow technology to dictate the rhythm of our lives.

This doesn't mean that we need to ditch all technology and go back to the agrarian ways of our ancestors. It does, however, mean that the path to holiness in the contemporary world requires us to step back and examine how technologies are influencing our physical and mental well-being. Addictions in any form can lead to destruction. We're used to seeing lives ruined by drugs, alcohol, or gambling. But how aware are we of those around us whose lives are being devastated by digital addictions? They may appear subtle on the surface, but like any insidious addiction, it spreads like a cancer until it consumes us completely.

This is where Leviticus can help. The festival calendar that God established for his people, and that has taken on its own form in the Christian church, offers a pattern of sacred interruptions in our lives to celebrate God's works of salvation. Festivals are meant to bring us together as families and communities of faith to offer prayers of repentance, thanksgiving, and praise. There are no goals to achieve in holy time, but life is suspended for the sake of worship and celebration. These are the moments we consecrate as God invites us into his holy presence for a foretaste of eternity and his coming kingdom.

6

Purity, Pandemics, and Purification

PURITY AND PANDEMICS

As we move further into our journey we'll discover that one of the great hurdles to understanding the world of Leviticus is grasping the concept of ritual purity and impurity. These are two categories of life that are virtually non-existent in our modern Western culture. When we speak of something that is ritually "unclean" in the Bible, we may conjure up images of something that's sinful or that God has rejected. We addressed this in chapter 4 when discussing certain foods and noted that there was nothing wrong or sinful about creatures that were unclean for Israel to eat. All of creation is still good and bears the glory of God's handiwork. Instead, we saw how particular foods would make Israel unclean *in relation to the tabernacle*. The barriers of the food laws were established to maintain the purity of God's dwelling *so that* he could remain in relationship with the people. The divisions were primarily for the sake of maintaining communion with God. The important thing to remember is that ritual purity in Leviticus has to do with one's relationship to God's holy presence in the tabernacle.

Some Christians see the purity laws as creating unnecessary boundaries that cause social division and separation. They might look to the many examples where Jesus shows mercy to "unclean" people and see this as the rejection of the Levitical rules. Jesus breaks down the boundaries that Leviticus created. This is a common misunderstanding and usually comes from a false portrayal of God as one who is only concerned with cold, heartless observance of his commands. Jesus, some might argue, demonstrates a religion of love and compassion that breaks the rules.

The problem, as we shall see, is that this is not how Jesus himself perceived the purity laws. Instead, he acknowledges the regulations of Leviticus but demonstrates his power over impurity and the forces of death associated with them. As Matthew Thiessen writes, "Jesus does not abolish the ritual purity system; rather, he abolishes the force that creates the ritual impurity in the person he meets."[1] Understanding ritual impurity in Leviticus can be difficult, but it's critical in our interpretation of Jesus' ministry on earth and in our ability to grasp how Christians experience purity and wholeness through the Spirit.

In the Old Testament we recall that when God's holy presence comes to dwell with his people there were certain rules established to maintain that holiness. Israel is to remain pure because God is pure. It's important to remember that many of these restrictions were not meant to last forever, as we see in the light of Jesus' ministry. As Baruch Levine argues, "The gulf between the sacred and the profane was not meant to be permanent. The command to achieve holiness, to become holy, envisions a time when life would be consecrated in its fullness and when all nations would worship God in holiness."[2]

This doesn't mean, however, that we can dismiss these commands altogether. The call to purity is very much part of the vocabulary of the New Testament. Just as ancient Israel was called to purity in a particular way in relation to God's tabernacling presence, so too are Christians called to an even greater purity with the indwelling presence of the Holy Spirit. Though the Christian is not bound by the purity laws of Leviticus, their institution continues to inform and shape our understanding of how to maintain purity in Christ.

Issues of purity and contamination may not have been at the forefront of our thoughts until the outbreak of the COVID-19 pandemic. This life-threatening virus has brought radical changes to the normal patterns of our world. Governments have enforced lockdowns, the wearing of masks, and physical distancing all in hopes of stopping further outbreaks. At the height of the initial pandemic the world came to a virtual standstill, paralyzed by

---

1. Thiessen, *Jesus and the Forces of Death*, 6.
2. Levine, *Leviticus*, 258.

fear as many nations did not have the medical resources to treat patients amidst a rising death toll. Those who had contracted the virus were "unclean" and separated from others in quarantine to prevent the infection from spreading. The pandemic has certainly reminded everyone of how dangerous the spread of a virus can be and the measures that need to be taken in order to prevent further contamination.

There is a good analogy between COVID-19 and the concept of ritual impurity in Leviticus. Like the measures that try to prevent the spread of a virus, Leviticus offers a series of regulations to help prevent the spread of impurity among the people to ensure the ongoing purity of the tabernacle. Just as COVID-19 can ultimately lead to physical death and the destruction of the wider population, so too did the Israelites believe that impurity, if left unchecked, would lead to both physical and spiritual death. This may strike us as some fanciful religious belief, but Leviticus reminds the people that physical and spiritual impurity are very real issues that have the potential to destroy the individual, the community, and to defile God's home.

When we first look at some of these rules they may not seem practical to us at all. How can something like touching a dead animal make you ritually unclean? Yet what doesn't seem logical to us likely made perfect sense to an ancient Israelite within the signs and symbols of their culture. Death was a powerful force that stood in contrast to the life, wholeness, and purity of God. To come into contact with death meant that the person was somehow temporarily infected or stained by it and was in need of being purified before coming back into God's presence.

The problem comes when we try to rationalize the purity laws and think of them only in terms of their practical value. This will lead to a misunderstanding of their purpose and intent. There certainly were some laws that had practical applications for hygiene or illness, like quarantining those with infectious diseases or cleaning houses with mold or potential infection (Leviticus 14). In fact, some of these verses in Leviticus read more like an ancient medical manual than spiritual instruction. However, the purity laws need to be read considering the symbols that helped form Israel's understanding of God and his holiness. As we move outside of the tabernacle to everyday life, we find that similar signs and symbols govern Israel's understanding and engagement with the world.

Leviticus is ultimately concerned with purity because it sees the world through sacramental eyes. If the people are to remain in the presence of God's holiness, then boundaries need to be created in matters of everyday life to preserve their purity. If his people remain holy, then he can remain in their midst. But if impurity spreads like a virus among his people and contaminates the tabernacle, then God cannot remain with his people and the result will be death and exile from the land.

The gravity of Israel's purity is summed up after the largest section of regulations which are found in Leviticus 11–15. God says, "Thus you shall keep the people of Israel separate from their uncleanness, so that they do not die in their uncleanness by defiling my tabernacle that is in their midst" (Lev 15:31). If ritual uncleanness is not addressed, what is at stake is the very holiness of God's tabernacle and his presence with his people. If God's sanctuary is defiled, then the final result will be Israel's death, because without God's presence in their midst the people cannot live in the fullness of his blessing. Unchecked impurity in Israel would be like a fatal virus spreading like wildfire without implementing any measures to keep it contained.

Though we may struggle with understanding the logic of particular rules around purity in Leviticus, we might recall that during the COVID-19 pandemic government regulations did not always make logical sense either. Though Western culture prides itself on following the latest scientific evidence, the statistics and analysis of the virus were often different according to various sources. There was not a unified "logical" response to the crisis and nations chose their own different approaches to containment. In fact, many turned to social media rumors and other advice that had no foundation in empirical evidence at all. So before we are too quick to judge the ancient Israelites for their beliefs, which may seem strange to us, we might take a closer look at how the world responded to COVID-19 to see that some of our actions around contamination and infection don't make much sense either.

UNDERSTANDING THE SYMBOLS

Though some purity laws in Leviticus may promote good hygiene, the majority are shaped by cultural beliefs and practices. Mary Douglas writes about the patterns and symbols created in cultures that form according to the inner logic and social order of society. Almost all cultures have rules around pollution or contamination, but they change from culture to culture. To understand Leviticus, Douglas takes a step back to look at the defining theme of holiness and writes, "To be holy is to be whole, to be one; holiness is unity, integrity, perfection of the individual and of the kind."[3] This is the goal for all creation in Leviticus—that all things might share in God's *unity*, *wholeness*, and *perfection*. She goes on to say that contamination, or the improper unity of two things from different kinds, leads to disorder and the breakdown of society.[4]

3. Douglas, *Purity and Danger*, 55.
4. Douglas, *Purity and Danger*, 95–114.

If we look at some examples we'll begin to see how purity rules make sense within the larger symbolism of holiness in Leviticus. In Leviticus 19:19 God commands, "You shall not let your animals breed with a different kind; you shall not sow your field with two kinds of seed; nor shall you put on a garment made of two different materials." These three rules demonstrate how holiness and purity extend to everyday agrarian life.

The first restriction on breeding animals seems to make sense. You might breed different types of horses together, but there is something that crosses a natural boundary if you try to breed a horse with a camel or a cow with a sheep. God ordered all life "according to its kind" in Genesis 1 as creation took shape. Each classification of species, both plant and animal, are commanded to be fruitful and multiply, but they must do so with others of their kind. The symbol of God's order in creation becomes the basis for how Israel should breed its animals. They should guard the wholeness and unity of creation by maintaining proper divisions between species in their livestock.

The second restriction on sowing two types of seed in the same field is concerned with the produce of the land. In some instances, planting two types of seed could be beneficial, like planting corn and pole beans together. The corn stalk can provide support for the bean vine and the beans add nitrogen to the soil needed for the corn to grow. This type of practice could be useful in subsistence farming where land and water resources were scarce. There is also the added benefit of reducing the risk of pests and diseases that may attack some plants and not others. The question of hybridization between seeds is not the problem since they would retain their own distinction even if planted next to each other.

In this case we see that the physical mixing poses no threat to the crops, but the symbolism seems to indicate that mixing two types of seed in the same field is closely related to the mixing of different types of animals. Despite the potential benefits of mixing crops, the symbol of purity and distinction are to be maintained in Israel's fields to remind them of being a distinct and holy people as they care for and maintain the integrity of God's creation. There's no apparent pragmatic reason for not planting seed together, but we see how symbols of purity and division in God's creation set the parameters for how Israel might cultivate the land.

The last command prohibiting the mixing of fabrics doesn't seem to make much sense, especially since some of the high priest's garments, and portions of the tabernacle, were made of linen and wool (see Exod 26:31; 28:6, 15; 39:2, 5, 8, 29). What's inherently wrong about mixing certain materials? Should we all stop wearing Lycra? Once again we need to think about the *symbolism* that forms the framework around these restrictions. Ancient remains show that knitting wool and linen together was common practice to strengthen fabric. The command seems to be directed toward the garments worn by laypeople and was possibly a way for Israel to distinguish themselves from their Canaanite neighbors. The outward sign of wearing something made of one material may have been yet another reminder of Israel's call to purity and not mixing with others. This might not make pragmatic sense to us today but within the symbolism and teaching around God's holiness it may have offered another physical reminder of Israel's call to purity.

These three examples governing daily life on the farm provide a framework for how we might understand the symbols that shaped the Israelite beliefs around holiness, wholeness, and purity. Though we might question how breaking any of these rules leads to serious contamination or chaos, within Israelite culture and its network of symbols these things were threats to the natural order of God's creation. The natural world belonged under divine governance and Israel was called to maintain its purity in every aspect of life. We recall that Leviticus sees the whole world through the lens of holiness. So whether it's what they eat, what they wear, what they sow in the fields, or how they treat their animals, all things in life remind Israel of their identity as a holy people in relationship with a holy God.

The symbols of purity extend beyond the world of farming to some of the natural physical states of the body and disease. In Leviticus 12–15 the main concern is not what *goes into* our bodies (like the food restrictions) but what *comes out* of bodies. Oftentimes bodily discharges are associated with impurity in Leviticus. Once again we won't always discover pragmatic reason for this, but we do see how normal bodily functions are thought to make a person ritually unclean. The following examples don't mention anything about a person's sin or the need for forgiveness. What is at stake is ritual purity for the sake of the wider community and the purity of the tabernacle.

In Leviticus 12 we find details regarding how a woman might be purified after childbirth. The command in Genesis to be fruitful and multiply was given to humanity so that they might populate and care for creation. The blessing of fertility and offspring is critical throughout the Old Testament and the birth of a child was considered a gift from God. Why, then, would a woman who participates in the act of bringing life into the world become ritually unclean?

The instructions say that a woman will be unclean for seven days if she gives birth to a boy. She must then remain in the "blood of her purification" for thirty days before making an offering to be ritually cleansed (Lev 12:1–4). However, if she gives birth to a girl, her time of impurity doubles to fourteen days and she must wait sixty days before bringing her offering (Lev

12:5). Some have interpreted this as a devaluation of women in an ancient patriarchal society, but there may be other explanations.

Most ancient cultures held different traditions and beliefs around the mystery of childbirth. Without the benefits of modern medical facilities, the infant mortality rate in the ancient world was above 40 percent. Childbirth was a dangerous event for both mother and child and was a constant reminder of the fragility of life. The close links between life, death, and significant blood discharge may have been the reason that ancient Israel linked childbirth to a period of impurity. Rather than seeing these restrictions as a comment on the lesser status of women in the community, we might regard these rules as protective measures demonstrating respect for the female generative power to produce life.

The doubling of purification time between male and female babies might also have been related to the natural process of recovery after childbirth. Post-natal discharge is longer after the birth of a female and the increase to sixty days may have been for the protection of the mother, who was still in a vulnerable state. When her time was complete, the mother could present her offering to the priest for her purification and was welcomed back into the fellowship of the community.

In early Christian tradition the requirements of Leviticus 12 were reinterpreted and influenced by the theology of Augustine. He argued that all human flesh is marked by original sin at birth, which results in our impurity. The only way for this to be cleansed is through the purification of baptism. Sadly, the Christian concept of original sin was then transferred to women who gave birth and so the church developed specific rituals for the purification of new mothers. During the medieval period the rites included ritual washings for the woman and being sprinkled with holy water by the priest at the entrance to the church. We recall, however, that the concept of the "sinfulness" of the woman after childbirth was not a part of God's original command in Leviticus. *Her ritual impurity was not a sign of her moral impurity.*

When we move on to Leviticus 13–15 we come to an extended portion of rules around skin diseases and discharges. These are the types of chapters in Leviticus that can test the perseverance of any faithful reader. The length of description demonstrates that these must have been significant issues that affected ancient Israel. In some instances, certain outbreaks had the potential of infecting the whole community, but in others there seems to be little danger posed to anyone.

Chapter 13 gives details around different skin diseases, which have often been translated as "leprosy" in our English Bibles. This is not a reference to what we might call leprosy today (or Hansen's disease), but to any contagious skin disease. For example, forms of psoriasis or fungal infections that included discharge or the peeling and flaking of the skin. Leviticus reads like a medical manual here where the priest acts more like a doctor examining patients.

As we have learned from the COVID-19 pandemic, the only way to treat infectious disease is to isolate and contain. Texts from other ancient civilizations show that quarantining whole towns or cities was not uncommon with the outbreak of skin diseases or other contagions. Most often these outbreaks were associated with the idea that the gods were striking the people with divine punishment. In Leviticus, however, the reality of skin disease is taken as a part of life and makes no mention of God's punishment on those who are infected. Other Old Testament texts make clear that leprosy can be a punishment from God (cf. Num 12:10; 2 Kgs 5:27; 15:5), but Leviticus simply prescribes the procedure one must follow to be allowed back into the covenant community. Enforced isolation may seem a harsh response to those with skin diseases in ancient Israel, but the intent was to prevent the spread of any contagion through the community.

In chapter 15 we find rules regarding bodily discharges. These can be anything from menstrual blood to nocturnal emissions or even sexual intercourse. In many cases the simple remedy is that the person needs to wash and will be ritually clean by the following day. Sometimes further washings and a longer period of waiting are required, which may be followed by offering a sacrifice. It's uncertain why almost any bodily discharge is associated with impurity, especially when there is no threat of contagion.

The rules may have to do with beliefs around procreation and the delicate balance between life and death. Human genitalia are associated with the production of life and an unnatural loss of blood or semen may have been associated with death and uncleanness. In the case of sexual union, the passing of semen to the female may symbolically represent loss of life for the male. The female may also be more in danger of death as the life of the child grows within her.

Sexual activity, reproduction, and new life were all endowed with God's mysterious power working through the human body. Leviticus does not try to restrict or control that power but, rather, it sets out rules that locate it in relation to God's presence in the tabernacle and the order of his creation. However we interpret the purity laws around sexual activity and the human body, it is clear that Leviticus treats conception as a sacred event that should be held with the greatest respect in relation to holiness and wholeness.

SEXUAL IMPURITY AND PRESERVING THE FAMILY

In the previous section we discussed the different ways someone might become ritually unclean. We remember that in many instances this was not due to moral sin, but to circumstances in life that can make a person unfit to approach the tabernacle and God's presence. The result of ritual impurity meant that one had to wash or wait a certain amount of time before returning to make sacrifices. When we turn to Leviticus 18 and 20, however, we find that purity is still one of the central concerns, but now we turn to sexual relations and purity within the very core of the family.

Though not grouped within the purity laws of Leviticus 11–15, chapters 18 and 20 deal almost entirely with sexual purity within the family, which demonstrates how important a topic it was for God's people. The fact that there are so many commandments around sexual activity within the household shows that it was a significant issue that needed to be addressed.

When reading the restrictions of Leviticus 18 we might be forgiven if our jaws drop. Were the people of ancient Israel really having improper sexual relations with mothers, fathers, aunts, uncles, sons, daughters, neighbor's wives, and even animals? The scandalous list of sexual activity might cause Hollywood filmmakers to blush. Was sexual promiscuity that rampant in ancient Israel or why else might Leviticus devote an entire chapter to proper sexual relations?

If we go back to the Levitical belief that crossing forbidden boundaries leads to destruction, then we see that these boundaries also relate to sexual activity. The Israelites are forbidden to "uncover the nakedness" (a euphemism for sexual intercourse) of others in the family. The underlying presupposition in these commands is that sexual relations are to take place within the bond of marriage at the appropriate times (i.e., not when the women is menstruating). Anything outside of this leads to impurity.

In chapter 18 there are fifteen commands against incest (Lev 18:6–18), which are followed by five prohibitions of other sexual acts or sacrificing children (Lev 18:19–23). The final section is an exhortation to be a holy people, unlike the Canaanites who lived in the land (Lev 18:24–30). We note that all of the commands are directed at married Israelite men, the head of the family. The underlying motivation for avoiding incestuous behavior is that Israel must be a holy people, unlike the Canaanites, who presumably committed such sexual transgressions. The outcome of the Canaanites' sin was that "the land became defiled" and "vomited out its inhabitants" (Lev 18:25) after God's punishment. The grave warning is a reminder that Israel should not suffer the same fate in their disobedience.

Much of chapter 18 is devoted to a list of family members that are barred from sexual intercourse. The prohibitions conclude with commands that concern sexual relations with menstruating women or adultery with a kinsmen's wife. The text then shifts to condemn sacrificing children to the pagan god Molech (Lev 18.21). This may seem puzzling to move from inappropriate sexual activity within the family to offering a child in sacrifice, but the command is probably linked to the cultic practices of the Canaanites. Though not much is known about the cult of Molech, we are told that Josiah destroyed a cult site in Jerusalem where children had been sacrificed to the god earlier in the time of Manasseh (2 Kgs 23:10). Though it is possible that "sacrificing" a child may refer to its "dedication" or "devotion," the practice of offering any child to another god, whether dead or alive, is completely condemned.

The following verse states that, "You shall not lie with a male as with a woman; it is an abomination" (Lev 18:22; cf. 20:13), which is then followed by a command not to have sexual relations with animals. Our initial interpretation of these prohibitions within the context of Leviticus is that they have to do with banning any Canaanite practices. Israel's neighbors had not maintained the proper order and division of God's creation and so were expelled from the land. Sexual boundaries had been crossed in unhealthy ways that had caused the earth to become defiled.

Stories relating to such practices are found in Genesis 19 with the men of Sodom and Judges 19 with the people of Gibeah, who had followed in the abominable ways of the Canaanites. In these narratives, same-sex sexual assault is condemned as a depraved response to the outsider.[5] Violence, sexual abuse, and lack of hospitality may have been characteristic of some gentile nations, but Israel was called to a life of holiness that is marked by love and generosity.

Same-sex activities that were related to pagan temples and Canaanite practices were also condemned. Moses commands that no Israelite son or daughter become a temple prostitute (Deut 23:18–19). It was not uncommon for male pagan priests or prostitutes to service other men. These activities occurred alongside the work of female cult prostitutes that were associated with Canaanite religions.

These practices were considered an "abomination" (Lev 18:22; 20:13). This word is repeated four times at the end of the chapter in relation to the ways of the Canaanites. The emphasis on sexual prohibitions, whether incestuous, same-sex, or with animals, all relate back to Israel being distinct

---

5. Judges 19 ends with a terrifying story of sexual assault by the Israelite men against an innocent female concubine, which is similarly condemned.

from the ways of the Canaanites. Israel must remain holy and sexually pure if they are to continue to dwell in God's presence.

The condemnation of same-sex sexual relations in Leviticus fits within its cultural symbols of purity and maintaining proper divisions within God's natural order. When sexual classifications are crossed, order breaks down and Leviticus sees this as a path leading to chaos. This is expressed in chapter 18 through the language of defilement and the land vomiting out the people (Lev 18:25, 28). The vivid image is like a person whose body violently responds to poison by throwing up. Such is the consequence of sexual impurity, which can lead to the destruction of the family and the covenant community.

We have spoken about interpreting the laws of Leviticus analogously with the contemporary world, but can we find a parallel when it comes to our modern understanding of homosexual relationships? It's important to start by going back to the ancient context of Leviticus, the purity laws, and the symbols that governed Israelite culture. The intent of chapter 18 is the preservation of the family by establishing rules around sexual purity so that they might not defile the land like the Canaanites. This may refer to pagan practices of incest, bestiality, or same-sex sexual activity possibly associated with the temple cult. All of these things are directly condemned by God as behaviors that should be banned from Israel's life. Instead, the people are called to holiness and purity to fulfill their calling as a priestly nation that reflects God's goodness and glory to the world.

What is being addressed in Leviticus concerning intercourse between men is the physical, sexual act, which is considered incompatible with God's holiness. It may be that male intercourse with other males was associated with forms of pagan worship and practices in Canaanite religion. It may also be that the behavior crosses sacred boundaries of fertility and reproduction. Male sexual relations do not lead to the possibility of bringing forth life and so may be seen as an act that defies God's natural order for intercourse between a husband and wife that leads to offspring.

Since the command against same-sex sexual relations comes after a series of prohibitions against incest, Leviticus establishes some analogy between the two actions, which both threaten the breakdown of family roles and relationships. What is consistent between the possible interpretations is that certain sexual acts are inconsistent with the identity of Israel as a holy people set apart from the nations. Leviticus is not concerned with individual identity or personal sexual persuasions but, rather, it highlights the need for Israel to strive for purity as a community and especially within the family. As we have said before, holiness is not achieved solely by individual efforts but it grows through the community of faith, and the core of the community is the family.

The addition of Leviticus 18 and 20 demonstrates that sexual behavior is very much a part of the call to holiness. Just as God limits Israel's physical appetites by restricting what they can eat, or how they treat the land, so too does he limit their sexual appetites for the sake of preserving purity and wholeness within the family. Certain relationships within the household between adults, children, and even animals must remain sacred if the people are to enjoy God's continued presence. Restrictions on sexual appetites even apply within the covenant of marriage, since a man cannot have sexual relations with his wife while she is menstruating (Lev 18:19). In this case the desire for sex must be curbed for the sake of purity even though it takes place within the marriage covenant.

The commands around sexual purity seem to be working on two levels. The first is to protect the roles and identity of each family member within the household so that illicit sexual relations do not lead to the breakdown of mutual trust and love. The roles of father/mother, son/daughter, brother/sister are given sexual boundaries and limitations so that each one might grow and fulfill their responsibility to the others. The additional command prohibiting sexual relations between men (or with animals) is also to protect the purity and harmony of the family.

The second layer of meaning is tied to Israel's call to be distinct from their Canaanite neighbors whose practices led to the defilement of the land and to their expulsion. The purity laws around sexual behavior, like the food laws, offer parameters for how Israel can both satisfy and restrain their sexual appetites. God's holy people are restricted by the boundaries he sets so that they don't destroy themselves or their families by giving unlimited reign to sexual desires.

The commands around sexual relations in Leviticus 18 (and 20:10–21) are concerned with the good of the family. Like any human appetite, if left unchecked it can lead to personal and/or communal destruction. What is vital for Israel is to be a people who restrict their desires for the sake of holiness, for the sake of the family, and for the sake of the wider community. Individual happiness or personal rights were not a primary consideration in the ancient world. What was important was the peace and obedience of the whole household, whether that related to sexual relations, food, clothes, or even Sabbath rest. To experience holiness and the blessing of God's covenant called for peace first and foremost within the family.

This makes it challenging to find analogies with contemporary positions on homosexuality and identity. Leviticus does not condemn a person's inclination or attraction, but it does condemn a sexual act between men.

A male may be physically attracted to males, or a female to females, but intercourse is reserved for a husband and wife in such a way that contributes toward the blessing of the entire family and to procreation.

The question that arises in a modern context is can mutual, loving homosexual relationships exist in society that do not contribute to the detriment of the family? Can same-sex relationships that do not lead to procreation benefit the community? Can homosexual relationships without the physical act of intercourse be welcomed within the community of faith?

To answer these questions, and others, goes beyond the scope of our study in Leviticus, but we can conclude with some certainty that the laws around sexual conduct are concerned with limiting natural physical appetites for the sake of the family and preserving its purity and holiness within the broader community. What we learn is that God's people are not independent human beings with the freedom to satisfy any desire in any way they please, whether physical or sexual. As members of the covenant community they are called to live in such a way that brings about the flourishing of the family and the whole community of faith.

The commands for purity recognize our human inclinations but set boundaries for how those inclinations might be satisfied. To be a covenant people means that Israel gives up the right to act like any of the other nations surrounding them. They are called to holiness so that they might reflect a better way that leads to life and the blessing of all humanity. The restrictions of the commandments around sexual relations were not for the sake of bondage but for the sake of freedom.

BECOMING PURE

One thing we must remember is that impurity was never meant to be a permanent state. Though one might become contaminated by sin or by natural means, *the goal of the purity laws are restoration, unity, and wholeness.* God does not instruct Israel to condemn those who have become defiled, but to help them be reinstated into the covenant community. Though some may have used these laws to exclude others, their intent was to restore all of God's people into fellowship with him and with one another.

We have discussed some of the requirements of purification which often involved waiting for specific periods of time, washing, and offering a sacrifice. But one problem that adds to our confusion about purification and restoration is the translation of the Hebrew word *ḥattat* as "sin offering." Most English Bibles use this translation, but, as Jacob Milgrom points out, a more accurate rendering would be "purification offering."[6] The "purification" refers to the effect the offering has on purifying any contamination from the tabernacle and from the offeror so that atonement can be made.

If we read "sin offering," then we usually think someone has committed a moral or ethical sin and needs to be forgiven. However, this doesn't make sense concerning some of the purity regulations. For instance, we read that a woman after childbirth is considered unclean and is instructed to bring a *ḥattat* to the tabernacle (Lev 12:6). We noted previously that the woman hasn't committed a sin by having a child, but her body was thought to be in a state of impurity because of blood discharge. Rather than making a "sin offering," it makes more sense to think of a new mother making a purification offering to demonstrate her acceptance back into the presence of God. Likewise, a person healed of a skin disease or a person with a bodily discharge is ritually unclean and needs to offer a *ḥattat* (Lev 14:19; 15:5). In these examples, it doesn't make sense to think of natural bodily occurrences as sinful but, rather, they are normal life events that require purification.

For Leviticus, the lives we lead are in a constant state of flux between purity and impurity. Holiness is never a static concept. We are all called to be holy as God is holy, but in the process we wade through the messiness of our physical world. It's in everyday life that dust and grime cover our feet. Our physical bodies are to be celebrated, but they can also become impure. There's nothing wrong with that and Leviticus doesn't condemn people for becoming unclean. What Leviticus does, however, is offer the guidelines for how to clean off that dust and grime before approaching the purity and holiness of God's home.

It might be helpful to think about ritual impurity and becoming clean in Leviticus by analogy. Imagine that you're going to visit your aunt Suzie's farm with your young children. When you arrive you discover that aunt Suzie has redecorated her home and (for some unknown reason) has decided to do everything in white. White carpet, white furniture, white curtains, everything white. When you arrive you send the kids off to play and she carefully instructs you on where you can put your shoes and hang your coats so that no dirt enters the house. A few hours later your children knock at the door and they're covered from head to toe in cow manure. They've been rolling around in the fields and now they stink. You're terrified that they'll destroy the house, but aunt Suzie comes over calmly and graciously leads the kids to an outdoor shower. She washes them up, tosses their clothes in the washer, wraps them in white bathrobes and brings them to the table for lunch.

---

6. Milgrom, *Leviticus 1–16*, 232, 253–58.

Getting dirty is part of life on a farm. It requires the appropriate washings and cleanings before entering into the home especially if everything is white! Leviticus understands that life is messy and that we need to be cleansed and washed before we approach God's home. In the analogy above, aunt Suzie doesn't love the children any less for becoming dirty but she does want them to be clean before they come into her house. In a similar manner, ritual impurity doesn't always imply God's anger with his children or his lack of love. Instead, it demonstrates his desire to make his children pure so that they might continue to experience his presence and the beauty of his holiness.

Any analogies concerning impurity are bound to fall short and there are certainly times when Israel's sin makes them both ritually and morally impure, which arouses God's anger. This a frequent theme in the prophets, which is summed up by the voice of Hosea. Israel oppressed the poor, followed Canaanite ways, and yet still brought their offerings to the temple. Yet God responds, "For I desire steadfast love and not sacrifice, the knowledge of God rather than burnt offerings" (Hos 6:6). This is often misunderstood as a condemnation of the sacrificial system, but the problem is not with sacrifice. The problem is the unethical, violent, and adulterous actions of Israel. Offerings for cleansing and impurity cannot be effective if there is no repentance and the people continue in their sin. The point of the ritual offering is to awaken the sinner to their impurity in the light of God's holiness so that they might repent and turn to his holiness once again.

Later on in Israel's history, the prophet Ezekiel condemns the priests in the Jerusalem for their own disobedience. God says through the prophet, "Its priests have done violence to my teaching and have profaned my holy things; they have made no distinction between the holy and the common, neither have they taught the difference between the unclean and the clean, and they have disregarded my sabbaths, so that I am profaned among them" (Ezek 22:26). In this case the very core of the temple has been defiled. The priests had neglected their duties of teaching God's people about how to remain pure and so the temple was profaned by their negligence. The consequence was the final destruction of Jerusalem and the temple by the Babylonians in 587 BCE ,which Ezekiel links directly to the impurity of the people.

The purity laws in Leviticus were not a set of strict regulations that God burdened his people with to make them miserable. The instructions were to remind Israel of their identity as God's beloved and chosen people. He delivered them from death and bondage in Egypt and now, in their liberation, he teaches them about their ongoing need for purification in his presence. When they became impure through skin diseases, certain foods, or whatever, they were not rejected but they remained his beloved. The purpose of the purity instructions were not to exclude people from God's grace, but to provide a way for cleansing and atonement so that they might be drawn back into his holiness.

One of the most powerful encounters we see in the Gospels in relation to the purity laws is when Jesus heals those with skin diseases. Such a scene is briefly recounted in Mark 1:40–44 when Jesus is approached by a man who has been excluded from the covenant community because of his skin disease. He pleads to Jesus, "If you choose, you can make me clean" (Mark 1:40). We cannot even imagine the fear and shock of the disciples as the unclean man drew near. If touched, they too might catch the infectious disease and be expelled from their families and community. Their lives could be completely destroyed in an instant, especially if their rabbi, Jesus, became unclean. But rather than turning to run, we're told that Jesus was "moved with pity," which is a word in the original language that literally refers to one's inward parts, or guts, being moved by compassion. He could have remained at a safe distance and commanded the impurity to depart from the man but, instead, Jesus reaches out his hand, touches him, and heals him instantly.

According to Leviticus, Jesus would have become unclean, and potentially infected, by coming into contact with the skin disease. Instead of becoming unclean, however, the reverse happens and the man is healed. The love and healing of the Father is revealed through the Son as one who has been sent to bring wholeness to his people. Jesus, as the tabernacling presence of God's holiness in the flesh, cannot be defiled by physical impurity. In fact, what we witness is the exact opposite. Rather than becoming unclean, Jesus cleanses and heals through his power by destroying the outward physical symbol of death that bound the man with the disease.[7] If the tabernacle was the source of all life and holiness that flowed out to the people, then this is what Jesus displays through his encounters with others. The power of God in the holy of holies is now invading the profane world in the form of the Son who brings life, restoration, and wholeness wherever he goes.

Though the man has been completely healed, Jesus upholds the Levitical laws and tells him to go to the priest and make the offerings required so that he might be welcomed back into the covenant community. The details of this are found in Lev 14:1–18 where the healed person must go through a series of rituals to demonstrate that they can re-enter the community. The sign of purification comes through the blood of the sacrifice, which is placed on the right earlobe, the right thumb, and the right big toe of the healed person (Lev 14:14). The same ritual occurs in the ordination of priests and

---

7. Thiessen, *Jesus and the Forces of Death*, 43–68.

represents the cleansing of the whole person so that they might draw near to the holiness of God. The priest moves from the profane to serve in the holy space of the tabernacle while the leper moves from exclusion into the holy life of the community.

Here we see Jesus both upholding the commands of Leviticus by telling the healed man to be examined by the priests, yet not being obedient to the purity laws himself. Why? On a practical level, the unclean man must perform the appropriate ritual if he is ever to be allowed back into the community of faith to live with his family and friends. Jesus himself, however, has no need of cleansing because in him is the power to destroy impurity and death. The legislation of Leviticus was not designed by the Father for the sake of exclusion, but for the sake of healing and making whole so that one might remain in unity with his holiness. In the same manner, the Son of God transcends the purity laws because he himself is the presence and power of holiness that can heal and restore.

This restoration inaugurated in Christ continues throughout the rest of the New Testament through the early church, bringing about the reconciliation between Jews and gentiles. This movement of salvation and purification following Pentecost was not immediately apparent even to the disciples. In Acts 10 we're told that Peter receives a vision as he was praying. He saw something like a great sheet descending over all creation and a voice telling him to eat (Acts 10:10–13). But Peter, as an obedient Jew who followed the food laws of Leviticus 11, responds, "By no means, Lord: for I have never eaten anything that is profane or unclean" (10:14). Though Christ had ascended, and the Spirit had been poured out, Peter still defined the world in relation to God's holiness in the Jerusalem temple. His world was shaped by the purity laws of Leviticus until he meets a man called Cornelius, a gentile in the Roman army.

Peter's encounter with Cornelius is one of the critical moments in Acts when God reveals the mission of his kingdom to purify and unite *all* people in the holiness of Christ. Up until this point, the primary converts to the gospel had been Jews, but the time would come when the message of salvation would reach the gentiles in full force. The encounter offers both a historical witness and theological imperative that gentile inclusion into the body of Christ was not an exception to the norm but, rather, it was at the heart of God's kingdom and mission.

Luke draws us into the inner chambers where Cornelius is waiting with his family and close friends. Though he is an unclean gentile, Peter agrees to meet with him and the others because of his vision and instruction from God. Cornelius tells Peter of his own vision and asks the disciple to speak to them what the Lord has commanded (Acts 10:33).

While Peter was speaking to him about Jesus of Nazareth, the Holy Spirit "fell on all who heard the word. The circumcised believers who had come with Peter were astounded that the gift of the Holy Spirit had been poured out even on the Gentiles" (Acts 10:44-45). One wonders whether Peter was just as shocked by what had happened. With a quick response Peter commands those who were filled with the Spirit to be baptized into Christ.

So critical is this moment in the history of the apostolic church that Luke repeats nearly the entire story in Acts 11 and then it is brought up for a third time in chapter 15. The purification and atonement achieved through Christ's sacrifice is now being implemented through the movement of the Holy Spirit by purifying and uniting all of humanity in the church. These New Testament communities would struggle with how to maintain purity and holiness in this new era of salvation as they looked back to their Jewish roots in the scriptures while also looking forward to a new covenant community united in Christ.

Though the rituals and instructions around purity in Leviticus were surpassed through Jesus' death, resurrection, and ascension, they had lasting value to Christians as they understood their own holiness and purity in Christ. Paul encouraged early Christians to live in purity and to strive for holiness. This was no longer about ritual purity in relation to God's presence in the temple, but in relation to the indwelling Spirit and to those in the body of Christ. Paul encourages the believers to be pure as he writes, "For God did not call us to impurity but in holiness. Therefore whoever rejects this rejects not human authority but God, who also gives his Holy Spirit to you" (1 Thess 4:7-8). Though the commands for purity in Leviticus have been superseded in Christ, the goal of purity is retained and remains central to the life of faith.

A similar chord is struck in Peter's words to Jewish and gentile believers as he refers directly to the commands of Leviticus. "Instead, as he who called you is holy, be holy yourselves in all your conduct; for it is written, 'You shall be holy, for I am holy'" (1 Pet 1:15-16). Once again we find that the language and symbols of holiness and purity in Leviticus are applied to followers of Christ. The new Christian community is held to no less a standard of holiness than were the Jews of the Old Testament. Instead, the Christian standard of purity has been elevated, since believers themselves are now a temple of Christ (1 Cor 6:19) and the church is the living body of Christ (1 Cor 12:27). Holiness in the New Testament retains the Levitical idea of separation and division from what defiles for the sake of maintaining purity in relationship with God. Christians are to separate themselves from the old self and their former patterns of sin so that they might experience union with Christ.

As the Christian church grew throughout the Roman world, Jewish influence waned as gentiles formed the majority of believers. The church refined its own purity rituals, mainly through the sacraments of baptism and the Eucharist. As people were accepted into the new covenant community, they were cleansed with the waters of baptism that united them with Christ and washed away the stain of sin and death. The ritual reminds us of the purification, healing, and wholeness foreshadowed in the rituals of Leviticus for those who crossed boundaries to draw closer to God's presence. Yet, like Leviticus and the need for ongoing sacrifices for sin, Christians also practiced a ritual that reminded them of their need for purification.

Through the Eucharist believers could offer what the 1662 Book of Common Prayer calls a "sacrifice of praise and thanksgiving." Consuming the body and blood of Christ is a sign of atonement, healing, and the forgiveness of sin. This ritual is an ever-present physical reminder for the church that the sacrifice of Christ has atoned for the sins of the world and has brought us into union with him and the Father through the Spirit. This is so eloquently summed up in the BCP prayer before Communion, "Grant us therefore, gracious Lord, so to eat the flesh of thy dear Son Jesus Christ, and to drink his blood, that our sinful bodies may be made clean by his body, and our souls washed through his most precious blood, and that we may evermore dwell in him, and he in us. Amen."

The purity laws of Leviticus may seem confusing at times, but their goal was to provide a means of purification that would restore communion with God. Jesus, the incarnate power of God's holiness, did not forsake the writings of Leviticus but, rather, demonstrated that he had the power to destroy the forces of death that caused impurity. Rather than becoming defiled, he healed, brought new life, and ultimately conquered all death. It is this power to conquer death that he bestows on his followers through the Holy Spirit so that, like him, they might bring purity, wholeness, and healing to the world.

7

Love Your Neighbor

Holiness, Empathy, and Artificial Intelligence

BECOMING HOLY AS GOD IS HOLY

In the last stage of our journey we come to the final section of Leviticus (chapters 17–26), which brings to a crescendo the call to holiness. Because of their thematic unity, scholars have often labelled this section of Leviticus the "Holiness Code." This is summarized by the command, "You shall be holy, for I, the LORD your God, am holy" (Lev 19:2). The call to holiness is nothing short of absolute. The end goal was for Israel to be consumed and filled with the very holiness of God. But how could the people achieve this and how can anyone, for that matter, be holy as God is holy?

We remember that in Leviticus holiness is a *communal* endeavor. It was not something that could be achieved on one's own but required a people living in mutual interdependence. A life of holiness meant that Israel was to remain distinct from the ways of the nations that surrounded them by demonstrating God's love, justice, and mercy. This required their obedience not only to laws concerning purity or sacrifice, but also to God's moral and ethical commands. They were to love and show empathy to their neighbor and to the stranger. The offering of sacrifices would never be enough to lead the people into holiness. They were called to love each other as God had loved them.

To be holy as God is holy is one of the great theological doctrines that emerges from Leviticus. Theologians often refer to this as the *imitatio Dei* ("imitation of God"). The rabbis understood this concept to be like royal subjects who were called to imitate the ways of their king. However we try to wrap our heads around becoming holy as God is holy, it's one of the most difficult verses to grasp because of the elusive nature of God's holiness and our own inability to achieve perfect holiness. Yet the command is also repeated by Jesus in the Sermon on the Mount. "Be perfect, therefore, as your heavenly Father is perfect" (Matt 5:48).

Holiness, we remember, is fundamentally about relationship to God and to one another. This does not change from the Old Testament to the New Testament. We see the ethical commands in Leviticus embodied in the life and ministry of Christ. Jesus' treatment of his neighbor, his healing, and casting out demons are all physical signs of what it means to be holy as God the Father is holy. It is through the life of Jesus that the fullness of holiness is revealed and we see the power of that holiness to bring wholeness and life. The Son reflects the love of the Father as he lives in obedience to the commandments found in Leviticus. Christ sets the pattern for all to follow and later as we look at the Christian calling to holiness, we'll discuss how this might guide us in our engagements with social media or digital technologies and how we might fulfill the command to be holy as God is holy.

In the first chapter we discussed the importance of Leviticus' vision of a sacred world inhabited by God. If we abandon the sacred, we are in danger of forgetting who we are as human beings called to holiness. Rowan Williams writes, "a loss of the sense of the sacred, a loss of the sense of being answerable to an intelligible gift, from beyond ourselves, in the long run entails more than simply the loss of God; it may entail the loss of the distinctively human. And if there is one great intellectual challenge for our day, it is the pervasive sense that we are in danger of losing our sense of the human."[1] At the core of Leviticus 17–26 we find the most basic commands for how we can flourish as human beings in our love for God and love of our neighbor. Leviticus reminds us of how to live within God's sacred world and what it means to attune our lives to the sacred through how we treat one another.

Leviticus 17–26 also emphasizes Israel's distinctiveness as a holy people. Their obedience to God's command sets them apart and draws them to his holiness so that they might be a "kingdom of priests and a holy nation." The call to be holy as God is holy is to be distinct from the world for the sake of preserving the world. Separation or division was not meant to lead to isolation in Leviticus. Israel was not being called to form their own community

---

1. Williams, *Being Human*, 25.

so that they could exclude everyone else. Their purity was meant to bring purity and life to the world.

To be holy as God is holy is for the covenant community to experience the fullness of God's purity and love. As the people draw nearer to his holiness, the more they begin to understand God's love for the world. And the more they grasp his love for the world, the more eager they will be to embrace the world and to share that love. It may sound paradoxical but the idea of being set apart as holy in Leviticus leads to a greater union with God, which, in turn, leads to a greater love for the world.

The command to be holy as God is holy was not designed to set the people up for failure. Though they could not be holy in all aspects of his divine holiness, they were called to a life committed to justice, righteousness, compassion, and mercy. This is why Leviticus is not merely concerned with ritual purity and things like what we eat, or drink, or how we worship. It is equally concerned with a holiness that's reflected in how we treat our families, our neighbors, our animals, the land, and even those aliens who come from outside the covenant community. The call to holiness is not about some sort of inner spiritual piety but, rather, it's measured in real terms by how we love and care for human beings made in God's image.

Leviticus 19 offers some of the clearest instructions on how to live in holiness through the love of one's neighbor. It's in this chapter that we hear Leviticus' prophetic voice that calls for obedience to the ethical demands of holiness. Just and compassionate treatment of one's neighbor, especially the poorest in society, is at the heart of chapter 19. When Israel failed to treat the most vulnerable with dignity and justice God responded through the voice of the prophets. We hear his condemnation reverberate throughout the fifth chapter of Amos.

> Even though you offer me your burnt offerings and grain offerings,
>   I will not accept them;
> and the offerings of well-being of your fatted animals
>   I will not look upon.
> Take away from me the noise of your songs;
>   I will not listen to the melody of your harps.
> But let justice roll down like waters,
>   and righteousness like an everflowing stream. (Amos 5:21–24)

Only when God's people walk in the ethical demands of holiness will he accept their ritual purity and sacrifice.

A common misinterpretation of the prophets is that they were speaking out against the sacrificial system and purity laws that God had established in Leviticus. The prophets are often seen as champions of social justice who denounce the legalism and ritual demands of the religious elite. This portrayal, however, is far from the truth. The prophets knew that ritual and sacrifice were critical in maintaining the purity of the temple and the holiness of God's people. They understood that proper offerings were required to ensure that God's holy presence did not depart. Their argument, like Leviticus, is that *sacrifice without ethical living means nothing*. Holiness and purity are only achieved when right living and right worship are bound together. One cannot stand without the other. This is one of the great contributions of the prophetic voices in the Old Testament. They remind Israel that there can be no division between moral and cultic purity when it comes to holy living.

The same is true for the church today. Christians no longer offer animal sacrifices, but we do gather in local communities to offer our gifts to God and to worship Christ in prayer, word, and sacrament. These things are necessary for the life of faith in the body of Christ. But if Christians turn and go out into the world to lead unethical lives, satisfying their own desires, and treating others unjustly, then their offerings of praise are worthless just as Amos says. To be holy as God is holy requires a life shaped by both moral and ritual purity. This was true for ancient Israel and it is true for the body of Christ.

LOVE AND EMPATHY

Leviticus 19 contains a diverse set of commands that relate to a variety of social and religious contexts. All of these, however, come under the overarching theme of becoming holy as God is holy. Whether it's obedience to the Sabbath day or allowing someone to glean from the edges of your field, the commands offer a framework for what it means to be set apart as God's holy people.

Throughout the chapter we hear echoes of the Ten Commandments: Honor your father and mother (v. 3), keep the Sabbath (v. 3), don't worship idols (v. 4), don't steal (v. 11), don't lie (v. 11), don't take the LORD's name in vain (v. 12). Alongside these are a variety of instructions that range from forsaking witchcraft to paying your workers their salary on time. At the center of the chapter we find the cornerstone of all the commandments that lead to holiness, *"You shall love your neighbor as yourself"* (Lev 19:18).

The command to love your neighbor as yourself offers a summary for the entire law in relation to how we treat others. A scribe once asked Jesus what the greatest commandment was and he responded first by quoting

Deuteronomy 6:4, to love the Lord with all your heart, soul, mind, and strength. Then Jesus went on to quote Leviticus, saying that the second greatest command is to love your neighbor as yourself (Mark 12:28–34).

There is much we could say about how to interpret the command, but, in some ways, it may be better to let the words simply speak for themselves. To love one's neighbor is to be able to demonstrate empathy for them as a human being. We seek to understand others, to bring healing, and to allow for them to grow into the fullness of who God has created them to be. This is what we desire for ourselves and what we hope we can bring to others. To love our neighbor is to be present with our neighbor and to demonstrate empathy as we come to know them and create space for them.

Rowan Williams offers an enlightening commentary on empathy in his book *Being Human*. He speaks about how we, as human beings, develop our sense of understanding and knowledge through others. Unlike Descartes' dictum, "I think, therefore I am" (as if we are somehow disembodied thinkers), we grow through our engagement with others, through the expression of ideas and mutual cooperation. This type of physical, emotional, and mental interaction with others is what shapes us as human beings. Williams writes, "Empathy, that is, the imaginative identification with a perspective that is not my own, is not just an optional extra in our human identity and our human repertoire, it's something without which we cannot know ourselves. Without identification with the other, I don't know myself."[2] Identifying with our neighbor is the beginning of love. If we cannot identify with others, we cannot love ourselves.

To show empathy to someone is to be in communion with that person, which leads to growth in our own self-understanding. Just as we consider ourselves to be fearfully and wonderfully made (Psalm 139), so too do we understand our ever-present need for forgiveness and mercy (Psalm 51). We are aware of our potential to become fully human and to live in the abundance of Christ and we see that same potential in others. Empathy allows us to live in such a way that we can encourage growth in others who are created in the image of God so that we too might grow into his image.

It's difficult to plumb the depths of the command to love our neighbor as ourself and why this stands at the heart of God's teaching. Some may struggle to love others and some may struggle to love themselves. Yet loving those who bear God's image is at the heart of what it means to be human.

We may find it challenging to love our neighbor, or those who are close to us, but what about those who are strangers? What about those who stand outside our communities or circle of family and friends? Here is where we

---

2. Williams, *Being Human*, 58.

find an even more radical command as God instructs his people to love even the stranger as themselves.

In Lev 19:33–34 the Israelites are instructed on how they are to treat those from outside of the community. "The alien who resides with you shall be to you as the citizen among you; you shall love the alien as yourself, for you were aliens in the land of Egypt: I am the LORD your God" (Lev 19:34). The Hebrew word *ger* is often translated as "alien, stranger, sojourner" and it usually describes a person who has settled in a foreign land but lacks the legal status of a native. This might have been a merchant or a tradesperson or someone like Ruth who was forced to move because of famine. The alien is a bit like a modern-day illegal immigrant without rights under the laws of a foreign country. Without a passport or appropriate documentation, aliens are susceptible to mistreatment, oppression, and injustice. The same was true in the ancient world.

The command "you shall love the alien as yourself" is remarkable in that it clearly echoes the previous command to love one's neighbor but now extends to those beyond one's own family or tribe. The stranger is the one who stands on the fringes of society with the hope of being welcomed, cared for, and protected. Israel is reminded that they too were once strangers who received no compassion as slaves in Egypt. The painful memory of bondage is to evoke empathy in their response to foreigners so that they might offer love rather than abuse.

To be a holy people means that one extends empathy even to the stranger. This requires Israel to reflect on their collective and historical memory of oppression and slavery in Egypt. Their former suffering acts as a guide for their treatment of the most vulnerable around them. Remembering one's pain can serve as a powerful reminder not to inflict pain on others, especially on those who are defenseless. Yet there is always the danger that the one who was oppressed forgets their past and becomes the oppressor. This happened throughout Israel's history and was frequently condemned by the prophets.

For the Christian, empathy for the stranger is also rooted in Egyptian slavery as we identify with the bondage experienced by our spiritual ancestors, the people of Israel. But the Christian is further reminded of the spiritual slavery we experience when we live in the bondage of sin. It is from this spiritual death that we have been freed in Christ. Paul writes this to the believers in Rome to remind them that they were once slaves to sin but have been raised with Christ. "The death he died, he died to sin, once for all; but the life he lives, he lives to God. So you also must consider yourselves dead to sin and alive to God in Christ Jesus" (Rom 6:10–11). The Christian memory recognizes both the physical oppression of Egypt and the spiritual death of sin as motivation for how we are to empathize with others and how we are to love the stranger in our midst.

LIBERATION AND CASTING OUT DEMONS

The demonstration of empathy that the Father desires in a holy people is rooted in historical memory. As Israel remembers their former bondage, so too should they be guided by principles of compassion, liberation, and restoration. The attributes of God revealed in the exodus demonstrate his love, mercy, and justice, which are further revealed through the life and witness of the Son. It is only in Jesus that we see can see the Father and comprehend how a human being might fulfill the command to be holy as God is holy. We could choose from any number of stories from the life of Christ that illustrate his reflection of the Father's holiness, but I want to focus on one in particular that demonstrates Jesus' empathy and power over the forces of impurity and death when he heals a man of demon possession.

Though demons do not play a significant role in Leviticus, they are mentioned in the ritual of the Day of Atonement as we discussed in chapter 2. We recall that the scapegoat was sent out from the camp to Azazel in the wilderness as a sign of bearing away Israel's sin (Lev 16:8). Afterwards, the Israelites were commanded not to sacrifice to "goat-demons" (Lev 17:7).

Demon possession was not a common occurrence in the Old Testament, but there are some instances where demons seem to play a role in the history of God's people. God sent an "evil spirit" between Abimelech and the lords of Shechem, which led to ongoing violence and hostility (Judg 9:23). The first king of Israel, Saul, was tormented by an "evil spirit" after God's spirit had departed from him (1 Sam 16:14–23). We also hear of deceptive spirits sent to confuse Ahab (1 Kgs 22:20–22), or the Assyrian king (Shalmaneser) who tried to besiege Jerusalem (2 Kgs 19:7). In these examples there is a clear authority of God over any evil spirits who operate in the world under his command.

In the Second Temple period leading up to the time of Jesus' ministry we find more examples of demons influencing human history through the rebellious angels that were cast out of heaven. According to the Jewish apocryphal book *Jubilees*, the unclean demons led Noah and his family astray after the flood. Noah prays that the demons would not torment humanity, but the fallen angel Mastema (i.e., Satan) pleads with God not to cast them all into the pit of condemnation. God listens and agrees to allow 10 percent of the demons to remain on earth to test humanity and be subject to Mastema until the time when they would all be cast into the pit (*Jubilees* 10).

Another important work of this period is the apocryphal book of 1 *Enoch*. This Jewish text details a heavenly vision that explains the history behind the fallen angels and their unnatural sexual relations with human women. These stories are based on the rather obscure events written in Gen 6:1–7. The outcome of this mixing between human and divine was the birth of giants (1 *Enoch* 7). Such a corruption of creation led God to destroy the world by flood and when the giants died, they became evil spirits that tormented humanity (1 *Enoch* 15).

Both of these works, along with others, helped shape the Jewish understanding of demons during Jesus' day. It is no wonder that the Gospel authors relate various occasions when Jesus demonstrates his authority over the demons by casting them out and healing those who were possessed. The coming of the kingdom of God is represented by signs of power and authority over Satan and his cohort. Demonic reign on earth was coming to an end, which was a clear sign of the Messiah ushering in the rule and authority of God's kingdom.

When Jesus comes to the predominantly gentile region of the Gerasenes, he encounters a man possessed by demons (Mark 5:1–20). Jesus has already confronted one demon at the beginning of Mark's Gospel who proclaims that he is the "holy one of God" (1:24). When the demon is cast out the people are astounded at Jesus' teaching, which commands authority in the spiritual realms. In the second story we are given more detail about the possessed man and Jesus' interaction with him.

The man has apparently had a long history of demon possession and has lived among the tombs where he could not be chained. Since he was too strong to be bound, the community had forsaken him to a place of death where he howled and beat himself with stones (Mark 5:3–5). We can hardly imagine the exclusion and suffering the man went through.

The literary artistry of the gospel author draws us back to Leviticus. Here we have a man possessed by an unclean spirit, living in a gentile region among the tombs of the dead, close to herd of swine. It would be hard to imagine a more ritually unclean place! It's also important to consider the detail of the man hurting himself with rocks. Though there are various interpretations, this expression of self-hatred and self-harm stands in antithesis to the command to love oneself (Lev 19:18). The setting and details of the story take on new meaning when read through the lens of the ethical and ritual commands of Leviticus. There is no way any right-minded Jewish rabbi would enter such an impure place, but Jesus does so to demonstrate the power of holiness over evil and his expression of empathy toward a stranger in bondage.

The demon does not leave the man initially at Jesus' command but responds, "What have you to do with me, Jesus, Son of the Most High God? I adjure you by God, do not torment me" (Mark 5:7). The "torment" the demon refers to likely alludes to Jesus casting it into the pit of condemnation mentioned in *Jubilees*. Instead, the demon begs to be cast into a herd of pigs and when Jesus gives his permission, the entire herd dashes into the sea and drowns (5:9–13).

Though the townspeople reject Jesus and ask him to leave, the healed man begs to go with him. To this Jesus responds, "Go home to your friends, and tell them how much the Lord has done for you, and what mercy he has shown you" (Mark 5:19). I'm sure the man wondered if he had any friends to go home to. Instead, we're told that he goes throughout the region around Galilee proclaiming all that Jesus had done for him.

To love one's neighbor, and the stranger, as oneself requires acts of empathy. Heeding the commands of Leviticus, Jesus recalls the suffering and bondage of God's people in Egypt. He remembers their pain and their outcry as generations were subject to Pharaoh's ruthless hand. In response, he goes willingly into the depths of darkness and impurity to overcome the spiritual forces that have bound his people. Just as the Father came down from heaven to defeat Pharaoh and the gods of Egypt to liberate Israel, so too the Son goes out to the places of death to unbind and to set free.

Many of us will not have had the experience of performing an exorcism. In most Western cultures the very thought of demonic possession is outlandish and sounds like fanciful tales of witchcraft or ghosts. Yet in many parts of the world demon possession is a reality of spiritual life and casting demons out remains a symbol of the power and presence of Christ's kingdom on earth. Whether we have experienced such things or not, the story demonstrates the power of holiness in the Son and his ability to cleanse, heal, and release. These acts are at the heart of what it means to love our neighbor, and the stranger, as ourselves. Jesus offers a visual, compelling reflection of God's deliverance in the exodus as he empathizes with those who experience bondage and loves them and sets them free. This is the power of holiness in the incarnation and, remarkably, Jesus invites his disciples to participate in same power as he sends them out to proclaim the good news (see Luke 9:1–6).

WHO IS MY NEIGHBOR?

We have seen that the demonstration of empathy is critical to fulfilling the command to love one's neighbor and to be holy. In the story of the demon-possessed man we saw how Jesus displayed empathy by going out into the darkest places of suffering to conquer the forces of death. There are, however, other ways that empathy can be expressed as a fulfillment of the command to love our neighbor as ourself.

In Luke's Gospel Jesus is confronted by a Jewish expert in the law who asks him what he must do to inherit eternal life. In response, Jesus asks the man how he reads the law (Luke 10:25–29). He then recites the first great commandment to love God with heart, soul, and strength (Deut 6:5) followed by the command to love your neighbor as yourself (Lev 19:18). Jesus agrees and commends the scribe, but Luke tells us that "wanting to justify himself" he asks, "And who is my neighbor?" Another way to frame the question might be, "To whom am I required to show empathy and in what circumstances? Are there some of God's laws that can be suspended so that I might demonstrate love for my neighbor?"

Jesus responds with the parable of the good Samaritan. Many are familiar with the story and in some countries there are even good Samaritan laws. These laws offer legal protection to those who help victims in need or, by contrast, require people to give assistance or be liable to prosecution for withholding aid. The story is often interpreted as an example of compassion that condemns the callousness and legalism of the priests who pass the beaten man by the side of the road and refuse to help. The love demonstrated by the Samaritan in caring for the stranger, binding his wounds, and finding him shelter expresses the true essence of God's love, which is greater than the law. This is the religion that Jesus has come to proclaim.

A more careful reading of the parable, however, seen through the lens of Leviticus, reveals that there is more at stake in the parable than might meet the eye. Richard Bauckham argues that the key to interpreting the passage is understanding the scribe's question in relation to the purity laws. "What the commentators have failed to see is how carefully and ingeniously the parable constructs a situation in which observance of a purity law conflicts with the duty of neighbourly love, thus posing the issue: which should take precedence?"[3] Instead of being a parable about love triumphing over legalism, the good Samaritan reveals a heated debate about which of God's laws are most important and which ones take precedence over others.

The scene is set with a man who has been attacked and is lying by the side of the road going from Jerusalem to Jericho (a route the priests often took). In approaching a dying, or possibly dead, man both the priest and the Levite risk becoming contaminated if they touch the corpse. According to the purity laws, they are not to defile themselves by touching the dead. If

---

3. Bauckham, "The Scrupulous Priest and the Good Samaritan," 478.

they did, they would then have to go through the appropriate washings and waiting period before they could go to temple (Lev 21:1–3). There may be a note of irony, however, as Luke tells us that the priest and Levite were going "down from Jerusalem to Jericho" (Luke 10:30), which implies that they had already performed their priestly duties at the temple and were returning home. In any case, the priest and Levite are presented with a clear dilemma; when two laws conflict which should take precedence?

For modern readers, the answer may seem blatantly obvious. The priest should love his neighbor and help the man even if it means risking impurity by touching a corpse. But this may not have been so crystal clear to Jesus' audience. The ambiguity around the debate between purity laws and other commandments meant that some Jews might have argued that the priest was right not to defile himself. It's possible that the Levite, with less responsibility in the temple than the priest, did not have as good a reason to walk by, but even he too was in danger of potentially becoming unclean. Yet Jesus uses the parable as a response to say that the love of neighbor does, in fact, supersede the laws concerning impurity. This is not a dismissal of the purity laws but, rather, Jesus is teaching how to interpret the commandments correctly. To love God and neighbor are to be at the forefront of obedience, no matter what the context.

The real punch of the parable is that the story is not about a priest or Levite who helps the man or even an ordinary Israelite, but a *Samaritan!* The Samaritans were generally despised by the Jews because they were a mixed people of Jewish and gentile ancestry that worshipped God outside of Jerusalem at their own temple at Mt. Gerizim. The Samaritans had their own version of the Pentateuch, but would have subscribed to the same purity laws as the priest and Levite. The inclusion of the Samaritan provides the shock value of the story because his response to the law is actually the correct one. Bauckham goes on to say, "His compassion is not some kind of alternative to legalism; it is what the commandment to love one's neighbour requires of him. He illustrates what it means to obey this commandment in this situation."[4] The underlying message is that even the most faithful and learned Jews have misunderstood what is at the heart of the law, but the unclean Samaritan has acted wisely according to God's command.

The question, "Who is my neighbor?" is complex when considered within the hierarchy of God's commandments in Leviticus. But the answer that Jesus gives is remarkably simple. Even a Samaritan, who was thought to know very little about the law, understood that compassion and mercy for those in need takes precedence over other laws. In cases where the

---

4. Bauckham, "The Scrupulous Priest and the Good Samaritan," 486.

requirements of the law conflict, showing love, compassion, and empathy to one's neighbor is of primary importance.

ARTIFICIAL INTELLIGENCE AND LOVING YOUR NEIGHBOR

We have seen that holiness in Leviticus is not merely about ritual purity but extends to our ethical treatment of other human beings. To be holy as God is holy is to be obedient to the whole of God's commandments, but when we encounter moments where laws conflict, the overriding principle of loving one's neighbor takes priority. To love our neighbor as ourselves requires empathy for fellow human beings and recalling God's grace of liberating us from death to life. Acts of empathy, like those shown by Jesus in the Gospels, are demonstrations of how loving our neighbor can bring about healing, freedom, and new life. It was through face-to-face, physical encounters that Jesus brought about transformation to those whom he met. Yet in a modern digital society, can these types of encounters be replicated in the virtual world? How can we show empathy and love for our neighbor in the online realm?

The expansion of internet technologies, and our time spent in the virtual world, has rapidly increased in recent decades. Many of us have taken little time to reflect on how technology is shaping who we are as human beings. We have been swept up in digital trends without questioning how they might be shaping our lives or our behavior. In recent years, however, some of those familiar with the inner workings of Silicon Valley have begun to question how our digital lives are being formed by forces beyond our control. This is especially the case with increased uses of artificial intelligence (AI).

Usually when we talk about AI we conjure up images of indestructible robots that have taken over the world in science fiction films. But the function of AI is much more subtle and is already operating below the surface in many areas of our digital lives. Corporations like Google, Facebook, Twitter, Apple, and Microsoft have been accumulating data from our online activity to feed into algorithms that mirror human intelligence through decision-making skills or mimicking human performance. The idea is that the algorithm is programed to track our online behavior to determine how we act so that it can "learn" and predict or influence our behaviors. The end goal for some of these companies is to develop supercomputers that can "think" and problem solve in the place of human beings.

In many cases these algorithms have been developed to manipulate and influence our decision-making processes. Whether on social media or browsing the internet, some programs are designed to track our user patterns to help encourage addictive behavior. The algorithms are fed massive amounts of user data that tracks every second we spend online. Every click, every like, every site we visit or search we make; all are processed by supercomputers which then compare our data to data from other users to determine what you might like or what might keep you engaged (i.e., addicted) to the platform.

Social media programmers learned early on that when someone likes or comments on a post or photo, it provides a small dopamine hit for the user. Dopamine is the hormone released in our brains that is associated with feelings of pleasure, but it's also linked to motivation and addiction. Thus the more likes, or whatever feedback it is that we get from social media, the more addicted we become.

The former vice president of user growth at Facebook, Chamath Palihapitiya, expressed his remorse for what social media platforms like Facebook have been creating. "The short-term, dopamine-driven feedback loops we've created are destroying how society works." He goes on to say, "So we are in a really bad state of affairs right now, in my opinion. It is eroding the core foundation of how people behave by and between each other. And I don't have a good solution. My solution is I just don't use these tools anymore. I haven't for years."[5]

The development of algorithms that process unfathomable amounts of data has allowed major online companies to exert their influence over users on behalf of advertisers. You might think that you're exerting your freedom when you chose to purchase something online or when you play a game, but is it really a free choice you made entirely on your own? Most of our online decisions are heavily influenced by what the algorithm recommends according to our previous choices and the choices of others.

The data that is fed into these algorithms may also come from text in emails or messaging apps. In 2004 Google launched its free Gmail service. Most people never read the user agreement that allows Google to scan every email for text that can be used for targeted advertising. Steven Levy describes the initial shock of users when adds popped up that were related to the content of their email. He writes, "By serving ads related to content, Google seemed almost to be reveling in the fact that users' privacy was at the mercy of the policy and trustworthiness of the company that owned the servers. And since those ads made profits, Google was making it clear that it would exploit the situation."[6] Wherever the data comes from, the corre-

---

5. Gizmodo, "Former Facebook Exec," (https://gizmodo.com/former-facebook-exec-you-don-t-realize-it-but-you-are-1821181133).

6. Levy, *In the Plex*, 172–73.

sponding response from companies like Google is to direct us to what they think we need or, more importantly, what their advertisers think we need.

We might choose a film to watch, a meal to cook, what coffee to buy, or news stories to read based on what is recommended. With a simple click we may, usually without knowing, be manipulated in our decisions not for our own benefit but for the sake of someone else's profit. What we think is our free choice is often manipulation based on algorithms that draw on our history of online activity in searches, emails, social media posts, or conversations in chat groups, to limit our choices to what the AI software thinks we should choose. This subtle modification of our behavior then directs us ultimately to what advertisers pay for us to see and encourages us in addictive patterns. The result is that our social media feeds or Google searches become so highly individualized and customized that we only begin to see what the algorithm thinks we should see.

Just think about when you perform a Google search on the internet. The top ten list of links have been determined by algorithms that want to steer you in a particular way. How many of us will actually scroll through to the ninety-fifth page of search results to see if we might find something helpful? Most of the time we chose from the first page of results, which means that the search engine is selectively choosing what it wants us to choose. It would be like going into a massive sweet shop with a vast display of colorful candies. Upon entering you tell the shopkeeper what you'd like and they lead you to one jar of sweets from a particular brand. You tell them you might like something else and they steer you directly back to the same jar of sweets. This is what algorithms and marketing do to us on the internet.

Not only does this happen when we actively search for something, but it's also being fed to us on web sites or in social media feeds. Let's say you post something on your Facebook account or on Twitter about losing a bike race because you got a flat. The next day you might see offers from your local bike shop on puncture-proof tires. Or you've done a search on how to lose weight and the next item that turns up is a 50 percent discount to join Weight Watchers or a coupon for a local health food company. But these algorithms are far cleverer than that. Maybe you do a search for an obscure Russian poet and the next advertisement you see is for a discount holiday to Spain. Why Spain? The computer has data from thousands of others who have searched for that particular poet and it turns out that there is a coffee shop he visited in Madrid that now hosts weekly readings of his poetry. This is how AI works.

This personal customization offered by algorithms stimulates addictive behavior by incessantly peppering us with advertisements in hope that we'll buy something and so that we'll continue using the technology. In his book *Irresistible: The Rise of Addictive Technology and the Business of Keeping Us*

Hooked, Adam Alter surveys the tech industry in relation to the programs and apps that have been developed intentionally to keep us dependent on particular products. Like some cigarette companies of the past that spiked levels of nicotine to ensure customer addiction, social media, gaming, and other online industries have used AI to keep us hooked to their programs.

Alter argues that neurologically there are very few differences between substance addictions and behavioral addictions. Both activate the same parts of the brain and are fueled by the same basic human desires. He writes that, "Behavioral addiction consists of six ingredients: compelling goals that are just beyond reach; irresistible and unpredictable positive feedback; a sense of incremental progress and improvement; tasks that become slowly more difficult over time; unresolved tensions that demand resolution; and strong social connections."[7] He goes on to survey the intentional ways social media uses one, if not more, of the list above to manipulate our behavior and create addictions through our online use.

Jaron Lanier, a Silicon Valley expert who pioneered virtual reality software, also discusses issues of addiction raised by adaptive algorithms that shape how we engage with social media. He writes, "The algorithm is trying to capture the perfect parameters for manipulating a brain, while the brain, in order to seek out deeper meaning, is changing in response to the algorithm's experiments; it's a cat-and-mouse game based on pure math."[8] He goes on to say that it's this type of programming that leads to behavioral modification the more we participate in social media. The result is that we, often unknowingly, change our actions or responses over time as the algorithm continuously adapts in order to keep us hooked.

Lanier raises the point not to say that technology or social media is bad. In fact, he's very positive about the good things that can come from social interaction online. Instead, the problem comes when social media and other platforms are manipulated by a business model that encourages addiction for the sake of profit.

We often forget that we, the users, offer something to these major tech companies through our online use. We use their products for free, but we also give them our data for free. They, in turn, take that data and use it to modify our behavior in order to create addictive patterns while using their particular apps or programs. All the while corporations make millions and millions of dollars at our expense. Lanier appropriately calls this the BUMMER machine ("Behaviors of Users Modified, and Made into an

---

7. Alter, *Irresistible*, 9.
8. Lanier, *Ten Arguments*, 15.

Empire for Rent").[9] This business model exploits our online data in order to manipulate our decisions and actions, oftentimes through misinformation, for the sake of profit.

Technology itself is not the problem. The issue is the use of technology to control people by tracking every possible ounce of data they offer online in order to make a profit. And much of our data is used without our consent. Shoshana Zuboff describes this as "surveillance capitalism," which she argues is marked by companies using free data for commercial practices that disregard human rights and encourage behavioral modification. "We are the sources of surveillance capitalism's crucial surplus: the objects of a technologically advanced and increasingly inescapable raw-material-extraction operation. Surveillance capitalism's actual customers are the enterprises that trade in its markets for future behavior."[10] The more that our lives are lived online, the more data we supply for companies and the more they continue to use this to influence and predict our future behavior. This is life in the digital age.

At the beginning of this chapter we discussed two of the most critical commands given in Leviticus 19—to be holy as God is holy, and to love your neighbor as yourself. We saw how Jesus fulfilled this command, but the question we must now raise is does our use of technology encourage us to live out these two commands? Does it encourage us to express empathy toward others? And this may sound like a strange question, but is technology helping us to become holy?

For many, the addictive behaviors and how we treat others online is, in fact, leading us in the opposite direction. Rather than loving our neighbor, we can get caught up in arguments and divisive debates. We embrace fake news fed to us by bots that further polarize our opinions and incite anger and division against those who don't hold our own views. We take to heart critical comments that crush our self-esteem and can lead to self-doubt or self-hatred. These are not uncommon experiences for those using social media mainly because that is where the system is leading us.

Social media, news feeds, or internet searches are locking us into our own personal echo chambers. The algorithms are optimized to predict and dictate what we should see which creates a type of myopia that leads to tribalism, division, and bitter partisanship. The political landscape of today is a witness to this very phenomenon. People are unable to communicate with others in empathy partly because they have no idea what personalized news or content someone else is receiving. This type of isolation can lead

---

9. Lanier, *Ten Arguments*, 28.
10. Zuboff, *The Age of Surveillance Capitalism*, 10.

to the destruction of relationships and communities if we remain unaware of how certain technologies are intentionally manipulating our thoughts and actions.

So how then do we fulfill the command to be holy as God is holy and to love our neighbor as ourself in the virtual world? Part of the answer lies in understanding the nature of the technologies that we have embraced. Connecting with others through social media holds the possibility of positive encounters where we might express empathy and love. But we must remain aware of the fact that what drives most current social media platforms is a business model based on addiction and behavioral modification. The danger is that a few tech companies have a concentration of power that influences who we are becoming as human beings and as a society. As their algorithms track our every action for the sake of increasing our usage or selling us something from their advertisers, many people feel less connected and even a heightened sense of isolation.[11]

One response may be to protest the behavioral modification techniques used by these companies by deleting our social media accounts all together and joining other platforms that aren't driven by tracking our data for financial means. Though this may be a difficult option for some, it may be what is needed to change the current system.[12]

We recall the parable of the good Samaritan and Jesus' lesson of how loving our neighbor takes precedence over other commands. If we take the same approach to social media and our online engagement, we might resist posting that negative comment or retweeting a divisive story. We might try to build others up rather than tearing them down. The tone of our engagement might change from amplifying negative emotions to promoting those things that bring about reconciliation and highlight the goodness of God's kingdom in the world.

Throughout this book we have seen how Leviticus views the world through the lens of the sacred, where all life, especially human life, has intrinsic value. We see this through the sacrificial commands, the purity laws, and the ethical imperatives to love our neighbor, and the stranger, as ourself. In a secularized and digital world that has minimized the value of human beings for the sake of profit, we stand at a crossroads in terms of which path we will choose. Will we allow technology to shape who we are and what we are becoming as human beings? Will we allow the virtual world to dictate how we treat others or how we behave in the physical world? Or can we

---

11. Shakya and Christakis, "Association of Facebook Use with Compromised Well-Being," 203–11.
12. See Lanier, *Ten Arguments*.

learn from Leviticus and begin to see the sacredness of Christ's kingdom as it can be expressed in the physical and virtual world?

In 2017 Facebook revised its vision statement and wrote that the company's goals were "To give people the power to build community and bring the world closer together." It's a lofty ambition to claim to empower every human being on the planet with the ability to shape social communities. The problem is that the statement assumes that people are somehow disempowered, disconnected, and living in social isolation. Yet Facebook claims it can remedy this through its software. They offer the promise of a connected social life that brings peace and harmony, which begins to sound more like a new religion than a software corporation that makes billions of dollars off of user addiction and data.[13]

Leviticus, however, calls us to different way of life. It calls us back to what is sacred, to what is holy, and to the presence of God in all things. Leviticus helps us to interpret signs and symbols. It opens up windows into the Christian call to holiness where we as individuals and as the church become temples of Christ's holiness in the world. These are the physical manifestations and signs of God's presence in our midst. The concern of Leviticus was for the purity of the tabernacle where God dwelt. The concern of the church is for the purification of the whole world where God is making himself known through every believer and the corporate body of Christ.

THE BEGINNING OF THE JOURNEY

Though we have come to the end of our journey through Leviticus, it is really the beginning of another journey in the continued exploration of the Scriptures. Attempting to see through the lens of the ancient biblical authors is no easy thing. There are vast cultural and historical chasms to cross, but the more we learn about their world, the more we see the unending depths of God's wisdom in Scripture that is revealed anew to every generation.

We have seen how God, by his grace, delivered a people from death in Egypt so that they might live in his holiness in the promised land. The commandments he gave to Moses at Mt. Sinai were for life, purity, and to help Israel fulfill their calling as a kingdom of priests. By following God's prescriptions they would be planted like a tree in the land, producing the fruit of justice, mercy, righteousness, and holiness. This would be a witness to all the nations that there is only one God and that he has laid out the path for true life and blessing.

---

13. Lanier, *Ten Arguments*, 132–33.

Yet for a largely illiterate population of former slaves, God chose to teach his people through rituals, sacrifices, purity regulations, how to treat one another, and how to treat the land. He gave them architectural plans for his home, taught them how to eat, how to farm, and how to work and rest. He established a rhythm for life through the Sabbath and festivals so that families and communities could celebrate together throughout the seasons and remember what awesome works he had done to save his people.

In all these prescriptions, Leviticus offers us a vision for how divine holiness inhabits the world and how the people of God respond to that holiness. This is why the path to holiness is all-consuming. It encompasses every aspect of life because all life is sacred. In the end, holiness is not about purity for purity's sake. Holiness allows each person to draw near to the living God and remain in relationship with him. And the more that the whole community of faith draws near to his holiness, the more they are transformed by his love for all life and for all creation.

Leviticus marks a time when the course of history was dramatically altered by the arrival of God's presence on earth. His glory made manifest in the tabernacle required a new covenant, a binding contract between him and his people. Israel was no longer a people enslaved by Pharaoh, but they were children of God and called to be his witness and his servants.

The story of Israel in the Old Testament and in Leviticus is also the story of every Christian. By grace we have been delivered from death and slavery to enter into a new covenant with Christ. Like Israel, new believers become a family of faith, the body of Christ, that is his witness to the nations. And like Israel, Christians are called to be a kingdom of priests and a holy nation (1 Pet 2:9) bringing God's transformative power, creative imagination, and life-giving breath to the world.

This faith is lived not in word only, but also in sacrament. Christians discover the deep symbols of sacrifice, purity, and holiness in Leviticus and how these things have been further revealed in Christ. We are invited to re-sacralize the world by opening our eyes to God's presence around us in all things, even if a secular society chooses to ignore it. Leviticus reminds us that the world is sacred and that the movement toward holiness was always meant to be a movement toward the consecration of all things. What Leviticus envisaged in the Old Testament is ultimately fulfilled in the final revelation at the end of time.

> And I heard a loud voice from the throne saying,
> "See, the *tabernacle* of God is among mortals,
> and he will *tabernacle* with them
> and they will be his peoples,

> and God himself will be with them as their God.
> And he will wipe away every tear from their eyes.
> Death will be no more;
> mourning and crying and pain will be no more,
> for the first things have passed away."
> (Rev 21:3–4, my translation)

I have italicized the noun "tabernacle" and the verb "to tabernacle/dwell" to show the play on words in the original Greek. The use here immediately draws us back to Leviticus and the first tabernacle where God dwelt among the Israelites. In the Old Testament, the people were still surrounded by the forces of death that led to sin and impurity, but the Revelation of John looks to a time when death will be no more. There will be no more impurity, no more disease, or suffering because God's holiness will be fully revealed. Then will we be able to live with him and he with us.

Revelation 21 reveals the end goal of holiness and the life God sets out for his people in Leviticus. Though they could not experience it to the full, the Israelites were given glimpses and a foretaste of the heavenly reality of God's kingdom and presence on earth. So too is the church given a window into the mystery of Christ's sacrifice and atonement for all creation through the outpouring of the Holy Spirit and the celebration of the Eucharist. What Leviticus longed for is revealed in Christ and the Spirit through the consecration of all things. The church is now the living temple of Christ's presence on earth and though we still reckon with the forces of death around us, we await and prepare for a coming king who will ultimately make his home with us.

Leviticus offers us God's guide to holiness that is fundamentally about relationship—to love God, to love our neighbor, and to experience his love for all creation. This came to an ancient people in a distant land with different customs than our own. They were given signs, symbols, rituals, and commands to help them understand who God is and the nature of his holiness. It's our job today to interpret those signs through the Scriptures and through the life and witness of Christ.

What is clear is that the call to holiness in Leviticus remains consistent throughout the entire Bible. To follow God requires devoting one's whole life to purity through obedience to his commands. And this obedience has been made possible through the Son and the Spirit who write these commands on the heart (Jer 31:33). Whether through the sacraments, giving offerings, caring for the poor, working the land, eating, or welcoming the stranger, every aspect of life becomes can become an act of holy living that draws us closer to his presence.

Though we may find ourselves amidst a secular culture that has been stripped of the sacred, the book of Leviticus invites to re-baptize our imaginations and to witness God's presence around us. Leviticus reminds us that the whole earth is filled with God's glory and now, through Christ and the Holy Spirit, all things are being consecrated in him. And he has invited us to enter into this holy communion. Through Christ and the Spirit we draw near to the Father and witness his presence in this world. Like Moses, we take off our sandals as we begin to see Christ in all things, in all people, and realize that we are ever standing on holy ground.

For Reflection or Discussion

CHAPTER 1

1. What can happen when we trivialize or neglect God's holiness in the world?
2. How might seeing the world as sacred help us to understand a book like Leviticus?
3. The idea of division often has negative connotations. How might division relate to holiness in a positive way? How does the creation account in Genesis 1 offer a vision for God's ordering and dividing of the world?
4. What kind of words would you use to describe someone you think is holy?
5. What does it mean as a Christian to be called to a life of holiness?

CHAPTER 2

1. What kind of rituals do we practice in our lives? How do these rituals reflect what we believe?
2. Why was the symbol of blood so central to Leviticus? How does blood relate to atonement?

3. How did God teach his people through the drama of ritual? What are ways we can learn about God through ritual and drama in the church today?

4. How does the Day of Atonement offer a foreshadowing of the sacrifice of Christ?

5. How can we understand the symbols of the Eucharist through Leviticus?

CHAPTER 3

1. Why was sacred space so important in Leviticus? Is it still important today?

2. How might our understanding of holiness and sacred space influence our treatment of the land/environment?

3. How does Christ's high priestly role surpass the Levitical priesthood?

4. How does the institution of the priesthood in Leviticus, fulfilled in Christ the great High Priest, help us understand the role of priesthood in the church today?

5. How might we cultivate our experience of the sacred in our daily lives?

CHAPTER 4

1. Why do you think God established food laws for Israel?

2. What did food restrictions teach the people about God's holiness?

3. How do we treat food and what we eat as an expression of our faith?

4. How might we change our shopping habits based on the moral/ethical concerns Leviticus shows for food and the animal kingdom?

5. How might we eat and drink to the glory of God as Christians in the light of the environmental challenges we face today?

CHAPTER 5

1. What dictates our rhythm of life throughout the year?
2. Do we pause intentionally throughout the day, week, or year to consecrate moments of holy time and celebration?
3. What effect do festivals have on our understanding of faith? How do they help teach the faith?
4. How is technology affecting our experience of holy time? Are there addictions that we need to deal with?
5. How might we shape our use of technology to fit within God's rhythm for our lives?

CHAPTER 6

1. How would you describe something that is pure?
2. What do you think it means to be pure as a human being before God?
3. How might we think of the purity laws as healthy restrictions to our natural, physical appetites? How do we live out this same purity in Christ?
4. How do the purity laws help us reflect on gender, relationships, and power dynamics within the family?
5. How would you describe the Christian pursuit of purity in Christ?

CHAPTER 7

1. How can we aspire to the imitation of God in our lives? Does this seem like a possibility? Why or why not?
2. What does the parable of the good Samaritan teach us?
3. Has social media had a positive or negative effect on your life?
4. Has the internet or online technologies led to addictive or destructive behavior in your life?
5. How can Christians demonstrate empathy and loving our neighbor as ourselves in an online forum?

Works Cited

Alter, Adam. *Irresistible: The Rise of Addictive Technology and the Business of Keeping Us Hooked*. New York: Penguin, 2018.

Bauckham, Richard. "The Scrupulous Priest and the Good Samaritan: Jesus' Parabolic Interpretation of the Law of Moses." *New Testament Studies* 44 (1998) 475–89.

Berry, Wendell. "Christianity and the Survival of Creation." *Cross Currents* 43 (1993) 149–63.

Brown, David. *God and Enchantment of Space: Reclaiming Human Experience*. Oxford: Oxford University Press, 2004.

Brown, Jennings. "Former Facebook Exec: 'You Don't Realize It but You Are Being Programmed.'" Gizmodo, https://gizmodo.com/former-facebook-exec-you-don-t-realize-it-but-you-are-1821181133, 2017.

Browning, Elizabeth Barrett. *Aurora Leigh*. Edited by Kerry McSweeney. Oxford: Oxford University Press, 1993.

Brueggemann, Walter. Foreword to John G. Gammie, *Holiness in Israel*. Eugene, OR: Wipf and Stock, 1989.

———. *Theology of the Old Testament: Testimony, Dispute, Advocacy*. Minneapolis: Fortress, 1997.

Carr, Nicholas. *The Glass Cage: Automation and Us*. New York: Norton, 2014.

———. *The Shallows: What the Internet Is Doing to Our Brains*. New York: Norton, 2010.

Davis, Ellen. *Scripture, Culture, and Agriculture: An Agrarian Reading of the Bible*. Cambridge: Cambridge University Press, 2009.

Douglas, Mary. *Purity and Danger: An Analysis of the Concept of Pollution and Taboo*. London: Routledge, 2002.

Eliade, Mircea. *The Sacred and the Profane: The Nature of Religion*. Translated by W. R. Trask. New York: Harcourt, Brace and World, 1987.

Gorman, Frank H. Jr. *The Ideology of Ritual: Space, Time and Status in the Priestly Theology*. JSOTSS 91. Sheffield: Sheffield Academic Press, 1990.

Heschel, Abraham J. *The Sabbath: Its Meaning for Modern Man*. New York: Farrar, Straus, and Giroux, 1951.

Jenson, Phillip P. *Graded Holiness: A Key to the Priestly Conception of the World*. JSOTSS 106. Sheffield, UK: Sheffield Academic Press, 1992.

Johnson, Dru. *Human Rites: The Power of Rituals, Habits, and Sacraments*. Grand Rapids: Eerdmans, 2019.

Lanier, Jaron. *Ten Arguments for Deleting Your Social Media Accounts Right Now*. New York: Henry Holt and Company, 2018.

Levine, Baruch A. *Leviticus*. The JPS Torah Commentary. New York: Jewish Publication Society, 1989.

Levy, Steven. *In the Plex: How Google Thinks, Works, and Shapes Our Lives*. New York: Simon & Schuster, 2011.

McNall, Joshua M. *The Mosaic of Atonement: An Integrated Approach to Christ's Work*. Grand Rapids: Zondervan Academic, 2019.

Merton, Thomas. *Life and Holiness*. New York: Doubleday, 1964.

Meyers, Carol. *Rediscovering Eve: Ancient Israelite Women in Context*. Oxford: Oxford University Press, 2013.

Milgrom, Jacob. *Leviticus 1–16: A New Translation with Introduction and Commentary*. Anchor Bible. New York: Doubleday, 1991.

Peterson, Eugene. *The Pastor: A Memoir*. New York: Harper One, 2011.

Rosen, Baruch, "Subsistence Economy in Iron Age I." In *From Nomadism to Monarchy: Archaeological and Historical Aspects of Early Israel*, edited by Israel Finkelstein and Nadav Na'aman, 339–51. Jerusalem: Israel Exploration Society, 1994.

Scarlata, Mark W. *Sabbath Rest: The Beauty of God's Rhythm for a Digital World*. London: SCM, 2019.

Shakya, Holly B., and Nicholas A. Christakis. "Association of Facebook Use with Compromised Well-Being: A Longitudinal Study." *American Journal of Epidemiology* 185.3 (2017) 203–11.

Smith, James K. A. *You Are What You Love: The Spiritual Power of Habit*. Grand Rapids: Brazos, 2016.

Thiessen, Matthew. *Jesus and the Forces of Death: The Gospels' Portrayal of Ritual Impurity within First-Century Judaism*. Grand Rapids: Baker Academic, 2020.

Turkle, Sherry. *Alone Together: Why We Expect More from Technology and Less from Each Other*. New York: Basic, 2011.

Williams, Rowan. *Being Human: Bodies, Minds, Persons*. London: SPCK, 2018.

Wright, Christopher J. H. *Old Testament Ethics for the People of God*. Downers Grove, IL: InterVarsity, 2004.

Zuboff, Shoshana. *The Age of Surveillance Capitalism: The Fight for a Human Future at the New Frontier of Power*. New York: PublicAffairs, 2019.

Scripture Index

OLD TESTAMENT

Genesis

1	1, 10, 11, 63, 98
1:1—2:3	10
1:2	10
1:3, 7	10
1:28	12
1:29	62
2	10
2:3	11
2:15	43
3:24	41
4	11
4:1–16	24
6	1
6:1–7	120
8:22	77
9:4–6	23
14:18	55
15	6
19	103

Exodus

2:24	16
4:22–23	15
12:1	84
12:38	84
12:48	84
12:49	84
19:5–6	45
19:6	16, 45
20:11	80
22:1	84
23:9	84
24:8	56
25–31	40
25:4	6
26:36	98
29	46
35–40	40
40	6
40:33	76

Leviticus

1–7	25, 28
1:3–17	28
2	28
3:1–17	28
3:16–17	28
4	26
6:1–7	28
8	46
8:15	27
9	48
9:1	77
9:7	48
9:24	48
10	48
10:1–2	49

Leviticus (continued)

10:6	32
10:8–9	49
10:10–11	12, 46
11–15	97, 102
11	53, 60, 62, 65, 70, 110
11:10	65
11:20–23	63
11:29–31	63
11:41–43	63
11:44	64
12–15	99
12	12, 53, 99, 100
12:1–4	99
12:2	7
12:4–8	25
12:5	99
12:6	107
13–15	100
13	100
14	96
14:1–18	109
14:14	109
14:19	107
15:5	107
15:19–30	25
15:31	97
16	88
16:2–19	31
16:8	119
16:13	31, 42
16:16	30
16:21–22	31
16:33	27
17–26	114
17:1–9	23
17:3–5	67
17:5	24
17:7	24, 32, 119
17:11	23
18	102, 105
18:6–18	102
18:19	105
18:19–23	102
18:21	23, 103
18:22	7, 103
18:24–30	102
18:25	102, 104
18:28	104
19	115, 116, 128
19:2	14, 16, 113
19:6	65
19:9–10	8
19:18	16, 116, 119, 122
19:19	98
19:23–25	85
19:30	81
19:33–34	84, 118
19:34	118
20	102
20:2–5	23
20:10–21	105
20:13	103
21:1–3	123
21:1–11	53
22:32	50
23	76, 80, 81
23:3	80
23:4–8	80
23:9–14	80
23:11	84
23:15–22	80
23:29	87
23:30	87
23:33–36	80
23:39–43	80
23:40	88
24:22	84
25:23	85
26	50, 68
26:2	81
26:14–39	34
26:12	69
26:26	68
26:28	32

Numbers

6:24–27	46
9:14	84
12:10	101
16	32
21:4–9	32
25:1–9	32
28–29	76

Deuteronomy
6:4	117
6:5	122
8:3	61
16:13	88
23:18–19	103
25	9
25:4	67

Judges
19	103

1 Samuel
14:31–35	32
16:14–23	119

2 Samuel
24:10–25	32
24:21–25	28

1 Kings
22:20–22	119

2 Kings
5:27	101
15:5	101
19:7	119
23:10	103
23:19	85

Nehemiah
8:14–18	89
8:18	89

Psalms
51	117
95	89
104:14–15	73
118:62	83
119:164	83
133:2	47
139	117

Ecclesiastes
3:1	75

Isaiah
61:1–4	86

Jeremiah
11:13	85
32:35	23
31:33	17, 132

Ezekiel
22:26	108
45:21–25	83

Hosea
6:6	108

Amos
5:21–24	115

Zechariah
14:21	54

NEW TESTAMENT

Matthew
5:17	53
5:23–24	28
5:48	114
23	17
23:23	17
26:27–28	36
27:51	56

Mark
1:24	120
1:40	109
1:40–44	109
2:1–12	52
3:4	52
5:1–20	120

Mark (continued)

5:3–5	120
5:7	121
5:9–13	121
5:19	121
5:25–34	52
5:35–43	53
7:14–23	53
7:18–20	71
7:19	53
11:17	54
12:38–34	117
15:38	56

Luke

9:1–6	121
10:25–29	122
10:30	123
18:11	13

John

1:1–3	51
1:14	51
2	51
2:13–17	54
2:21	51
6:53–57	37
7:37–38	89

Acts

2	86
2:42–47	86
4:32–37	86
5:1–11	49
6:1–2	86
10	110
10:10–13	110
10:14	110
10:33	110
10:44–45	111
11	111
15	111
15:20	23, 71

1 Corinthians

6:19	111
8:1	71
8:19	71
9:10–12	9, 67
10:23	71
10:25–31	72
11:1	71
12:27	111

Ephesians

2:21	57

Colossians

1:17–20	35

1 Thessalonians

4:7–8	111

Hebrews

4:15	55
5:1–10	55
7:1—9:28	55
7:3	55
7:23–25	56
9:11–12	35
9:22	24
9:23–28	35
10:14	56
10:19–22	56
12:29	50

1 Peter

1:15–16	111
2:5	57
2:9	16, 131

Revelation

1:10	82
21	81, 132
21:3	82
21:3–4	132
21:22–24	82

PSEUDEPIGRAPHA

Jubilees

10   119

1 Enoch

7   120
15   120

www.ingramcontent.com/pod-product-compliance
Lightning Source LLC
Chambersburg PA
CBHW022122160426
43197CB00009B/1122